GREAT SPIRITUAL REVIVALS

COMPILED BY HAYES PRESS

Published by:

HAYES PRESS Publisher, Resources & Media,

The Barn, Flaxlands

Royal Wootton Bassett

Swindon, SN4 8DY

United Kingdom

I0201134

Table of Contents

PREFACE

———

REVIVAL! WHAT AN INSPIRING and uplifting word - and a word that is much needed today. As we read of examples of spiritual revival in Old Testament times, it causes us to think of ourselves and our need for the very same thing – both individually and collectively. May our prayer be that of the hymnwriter ...

Revive Thy work, O Lord,

Thy mighty arm make bare;

Speak with the voice that wakes the dead,

And make Thy people hear.

Revive Thy work, O Lord,

Disturb this sleep of death;

Quicken the smoldering embers now

By Thine almighty breath.

Revive Thy work, O Lord,

Create soul-thirst for Thee;

And hungering for the bread of life

O may our spirits be.

Revive Thy work, O Lord,

Exalt Thy precious name;

And, by the Spirit, Lord our love

For Thee and Thine inflame.

Revive Thy work, O Lord,

And give refreshing showers;

The glory shall be all Thine own,

The blessing, Lord, be ours.

(Albert Midlane)

CHAPTER ONE: CONCERN FOR THE ARK

———

IN THE FURNITURE OF the Tabernacle that the children of Israel built for the Lord the Ark of the covenant had a prime place. It was viewed with reverence because in a special way it signified the divine Presence among God's people. Even the Philistines, when they learned that the Ark had been brought to the battle field, exclaimed with alarm, "God is come into the camp" (1 Samuel 4:7).

Something of the significance of the Ark is traceable in the comment of the widow of Phinehas, the son of Eli, when she heard that the Ark had been captured by the Philistines. To her son just born she gave the name Ichabod, meaning, "There is no glory", and she said, "The glory is departed from Israel; for the Ark of God is taken" (1 Samuel 4:22).

The proper place for the Ark was the holy of holies of the Tabernacle, which was the house of God and the temple of the Lord. It was, therefore, an action of reckless insubjection when the people of God with the encouragement and assistance of two priests of the Lord removed the Ark from its place and carried it out to the camp of the armed forces. The consequences were in every way disastrous. Thirty thousand of the army of Israel were killed and the Ark of God was taken by the Philistines to be placed beside Dagon their idol god. What a serious travesty;

the Ark of God taken from the most holy place of the house of God and placed beside the image of Dagon in the house of that lifeless god!

But the Ark must remain in the land of the Philistines. God intervened with severe judgement which shattered those people. For seven months the Ark was in their land. They were seven months of bitter suffering. The anguished cry of the people went up to heaven until at last there was conceived a method by which the Ark could be returned to Israel.

The arrival of the Ark in the land of Israel led to another manifestation of divine judgement. The men of Beth-shemesh succumbed to the unholy curiosity of seeing what the Ark contained. Spiritual privilege and liberty are always governed by the claims of divine holiness. Genuine interest in the things of God must be commended and encouraged, but mere curiosity can only be condemned. Fifty thousand and seventy men died at Beth-shemesh. We draw attention to the words spoken by those who escaped the judgement, "Who is able to stand before the LORD, this holy God? And to whom shall He go up from us?" (1 Samuel 6:20). These questions emphasize something of the significance of the Ark and of the solemnity of dealing with what belongs to the house of God.

Eventually the Ark was placed in the house of a man named Abinadab whose son Eleazer guarded it. But of course the proper place for the Ark was the house of God, and the grave irregularity which had developed must have caused sorrow to the Lord. Then Israel was given a king. He was a young man who by his ascension to the throne was offered the challenge of tremendous possibilities. Spiritually the Israel people were in disarray. As a nation they lived in fear because of the recurring attacks of their enemy the Philistines. At the commencement of his reign Saul gave promise of better days for Israel. He manifested in his character humility, courage and a readiness to forgive. He had also available to him the wise counsel of the godly man Samuel.

Surely here was a kingly leader who would guide the people back to God and to the importance and significance of the house of God. On the contrary, it soon became evident that power, authority, wealth and influence had gone to Saul's head. He was not a spiritually-minded man. He had little interest in the house of God. It was of no concern to him that the Ark of God was in the house of Abinadab instead of being where it should be - in the house of God. In a later day David said of the Ark, "We sought not unto it in the days of Saul". This neglect gave a clear indication of the attitude of Saul to God Himself.

After Saul, a man came to the throne of Israel to whom was borne the divine witness, "I have found David the son of Jesse, a man after My heart, who shall do all My will". The Lord "chose David also His servant, and took him from the sheepfolds". We think of David as a young man caring for his father's sheep. He was a spiritually-minded youth, and it is reasonable to believe that as he watched over the sheep in their pasture he must often have meditated on the work and purpose of God in redeeming his forefathers from the bondage of Egypt and leading them forth to be His flock to follow Him and His people serve to Him. In particular David may have thought of that structure, erected by God's command and according to His pattern. That structure, the Tabernacle, was God's house, His dwelling-place among His people. There grew and developed in David a love for God's house.

As years went past it must have caused increasing grief to David to see the spiritual condition of God's people, and especially to realize that the Ark belonging to the house which he loved was not where it should be. The house of Abinadab chosen by men was a poor substitute for the place of divine choice, the place of the Name. Something of the deep inward movements in the heart of David can be learned from the words of Psalm 132, "Lord, remember for David all his affliction; how he sware unto the Lord, and vowed unto the Mighty One of Jacob: surely I will not come into the tabernacle of my house, nor go up into my bed; I will not give sleep to mine eyes, or slumber to mine eyelids; until I find out a place for the LORD, a tabernacle for the Mighty One of Jacob".

"A place for the Lord". There is much instruction in these words. There is a danger that those who have found a place in the sovereign purposes of divine love and grace may find their minds preoccupied with what God has done for them. They may be genuinely grateful as they meditate on the many blessings enjoyed on earth and as they anticipate what God has prepared for them in an assured blissful, eternal future. But what about the responsibility of response expressing itself in securing on earth a place for God, a place where He can rest? Let us hear again words from Psalm 132, "The LORD hath chosen Zion; He hath desired it for His habitation. This is My resting place for ever: here will I dwell; for I have desired it". God wants a house on earth, a resting place among His people, a place where

His authority is acknowledged. This was true in the past. It is true in the present dispensation in which it is God's purpose that believers in Christ should give to Him on earth the place of all authority that God has given to Him in heaven.

When David became king and thus gained regal authority, power and influence he quickly manifested the deep exercise of heart about the Ark of God. For a long time it had been neglected but the expressed concern of David and the example of his leadership led to a time of spiritual revival in Israel. We draw attention to some features of that revival.

For about seven years after David came to the throne there were divided loyalties in Israel, but eventually the whole nation was united in subjection to David. The people were of one heart. This unity was important in the development of God's purposes through David. Perhaps that was the time when he wrote, "Behold, how good and how pleasant it is for brethren to dwell together in unity!" (Psalm 133:1). Unity gives joy, and joy imparts strength. We read, "There was joy in Israel" (1 Chronicles 12:40). The people were now in a good spiritual condition to move forward in the way of God.

The vision of the house of God was vivid in the mind of David and there burned warmly in his heart the desire to see the Ark of God in the place that God had chosen. But he had no thought of acting in an individual way. He wanted and sought the fellowship of his people and the collective conviction that what he proposed to do proceeded from the Lord and was not merely the product of his own mind. The unity that joyfully bound the people together found expression in a ready response on the part of the leaders whom David consulted. He had placed before them, "Let us bring again the ark of God to us". "And all the assembly said that they would do so: for the thing was right in the eyes of all the people" (1 Chronicles 13:1-4).

A large and happy procession set off from the house of Abinadab to bring the Ark to Zion. But lessons had to be learned. Zeal is powerful and desirable but it must be governed by subjection to the authority of God's word and the acknowledgement of His holiness. Such lessons are sometimes learned through very bitter experience. This is sadly illustrated in the tragic events of 2 Samuel 6:6-9.

Eventually David had the joy and satisfaction of seeing the Ark being placed in the tent which he had pitched for it. But even then the concern of that great man of God was not fully answered, as will be seen in a subsequent chapter in this book.

CHAPTER TWO: GIVING FOR GOD'S HOUSE

A MOST IMPRESSIVE COMPANY was gathered. It was King David's last public appearance; the last time he would stand with his people before the Lord. He summoned all the leaders of the nation to be present, princes, captains, rulers, officers and the mighty men - they were all there. The men who had helped to make Israel great. Doubtless some had shared with David the rigours of his early days, when he was chased by Saul. They had been with him also through the years of his reign, sharing the glory of his victories and the bitterness of his defeats. Now David was an old man, and the time had come to hand over responsibility. The old warrior stood to make his final charge.

It was an occasion calculated to stir all present to the depth of their beings. The account takes up two chapters of 1 Chronicles, 28 and 29. The very sight of their aged leader was sufficient to move their hearts. A man of God from his youth, the stamp of the Divine was upon him. In boyhood, decisions were made which marked out the course of his life. As a young shepherd he learned to love the Lord, and that love grew until it became the all-consuming passion of his life. In early manhood he spoke out plainly, that all might know, "I love Thee, O LORD, my strength" (Psalm 18:1). Inevitably that caused him to love what the Lord loved, and in Psalm 26 he spoke again, "LORD, I love the habitation of Thy house, and the place where Thy glory dwelleth" (v.8).

9

We pause to enquire, is it so with ourselves? Do we love the Lord, and is that love directed by His Word, so that we also love the place where He dwells? A salutary question, and worth a careful answer in the quietness of the secret place. For as we shall see, the richness of David's life with the glory it brought to God was the direct result of the love which burned in his heart.

"Your young men shall see visions" wrote Joel the prophet, and David was still a young man when he got the vision of God's dwelling place and his own life of service in relation to it. 1 Chronicles 9:22 suggests that he and Samuel together ordained the offices of the Levites in their service in God's house, and Samuel died before David came to the throne. David was still in his twenties. Youth and age worked together, planning the orderly service of God's house.

From those early days it had filled his vision. Strength and affection combined to provide a dwelling-place which was as worthy of the Divine Being as human heart and hands could make it. As the old monarch stood in front of his people that day he reviewed his service in relation to this great desire. "It was in my heart to build a house of rest for the Ark of the Covenant of the LORD". That is where it all began - in David's heart.

Briefly he went over it all: his great desire to build, God's gentle refusal and His choice of Solomon for the task. Then he addressed himself to Solomon, charging him to know the God of his father, and to serve Him with a perfect heart and a willing mind. Weighty indeed are the words of verses 9 and 10 of 1 Chronicles 28, which any young man or woman stretching forward to the service of the Lord might well take to heart.

Giving is very much in evidence in the two chapters of our study, and in each case that which was given was first received from the Lord; whether it was David's wise counsel, fruit of his long experience with God, or the pattern of the house which he had been made to understand in writing from the hand of the Lord, or the materials which he had provided. In each case it was true that "all things come of Thee, and of Thine own have we given Thee" (29:14). But it is equally true that God holds men responsible to provide what He has given and to work with it, and in this there could be no finer example than David.

"Whatsoever thy hand findeth to do, do it with thy might" (Ecclesiastes 9:10) is advice which may well have come from David in the first place. Certainly he put all his might into the formidable task before him, and nothing was overlooked, from wrought stones hewn by masons to iron nails for the doors; gold, silver, brass, iron and wood, each had its own place, as well as all manner of precious stones. "Abundance" and "abundantly" are words predominant in the sacred account, as though the Spirit of God would emphasize David's generosity.

All this preparation was from national treasure, the wealth of the land and perhaps the spoils of war, but David was not satisfied. 1 Chronicles 29:3 is very touching. "Moreover also, because I have set my affection to the house of my God, seeing that I have a treasure of mine own of gold and silver, I give it unto the house of my God, over and above all that I have prepared for the holy house". "A treasure of mine own". It was his to keep had he so wished. But David did not view it that way. It was his to give. So deep was his love that nothing was held back. No sacrifice was considered too great. The Lord was worthy of his best, and

David gave it, over and above all that he had prepared. And it is interesting to notice that the gold and silver of David's personal gift was used to beautify God's house. The walls of the houses were overlaid with it.

We pause to contemplate such outstanding devotion. Surely we must, for its lesson speaks loudly to our hearts. We think of another day, in God's spiritual house, and of the grace that was given in the churches of Macedonia. They were building for God too, and Paul bears witness to the riches of their liberality, that beyond their power they gave of their own accord. And their secret was that first they gave their own selves to the Lord. "Their own selves", a treasure of their own indeed, to keep for themselves or to give to the Lord! Such devotion beautifies God's house. There is no doubt about that. They were days of abundance, despite their deep poverty. Abundant joy resulting in abundant liberality and in the churches of Macedonia there was abundant blessing also.

This sort of giving affects others. Paul referred to it for the encouragement of the Corinthian saints. God used it in David's case to stir the hearts of the leaders. David did not ask for their money. He asked for their hearts. "Who then offereth willingly to consecrate himself this day unto the LORD?" The Spirit of God was at work that day. Princes, captains and rulers, they all offered willingly. And the proof that their hearts were moved was the treasure they poured into God's house.

And more than that, for as the leaders took the lead in Israel the people also offered themselves willingly. Great days they were. There was no constraint, except that gentle constraint which the

Holy Spirit puts upon our spirits when He begins to work. And the result was a willing offering of themselves with a heart that was perfect, in the sense of undivided. There was no division of loyalties. They were the Lord's and all that they had was His, for the building of His house, and the forward progress of His work.

It was great spiritual revival and characterized by a deep joy in the Lord, as revival always is. "The people rejoiced ... and David the king rejoiced with great joy" Their joy flowed out to one another and upward to God in a volume of praise which glorified His name. Our own hearts warm at the contemplation of it, and we cannot but long for similar movements of God's Spirit today. We suggest that a study of David's prayer (1 Chronicles 29:10-19) may well reveal some of the basic conditions for which God looks if He is to visit us with revival. We list them for our careful and prayerful consideration.

1. All the glory was given to God. David was most emphatic on this point. In verses 11 to 13 he repeatedly gives the glory to God. "Thine, O LORD, is the greatness, and the power, and the glory, and the victory, and the majesty".

2. They had lowly thoughts of themselves. He carried his people with him when he said, "who am I, and what is my people, that we should be able to offer so willingly after this sort?" "Our days on earth are as a shadow, and there is no abiding". This is an important point, for God works with the lowly in heart. "To this man will I look, even to him that is poor and of a

contrite spirit"... "to revive the spirit of the humble, and to revive the heart of the contrite ones" (Isaiah 66:2; 57:15).

3. Their hearts were sensitive to the word of God, resulting in a willingness to obey it implicitly. "Give unto Solomon my son a perfect heart, to keep Thy commandments, Thy testimonies, and Thy statutes." Love for God and obedience to His word always go hand in hand.

4. An awareness of the holiness of God and His abhorrence of sin. David had learned that the Lord searches all hearts and understands all the imaginations of the thoughts. There can be no hiding from Him. "I know also, my God, that Thou triest the heart, and has pleasure in uprightness" (v.17).

5. A willingness to yield the heart and life to God. Is this too high a price to pay? David did not think so, nor his people. Shall we not also offer willingly after this sort, and with the sons of Korah pray, "Wilt Thou not quicken us again: that Thy people may rejoice in Thee?" (Psalm 85:6).

CHAPTER THREE: THE GLORY OF SOLOMON'S TEMPLE

———

FOR ABOUT FIVE HUNDRED years, God's dwelling-place had been the Tabernacle, constructed in the wilderness by a willing-hearted people in strict accordance with a divinely-given pattern. This portable structure was uniquely suited to the needs of a pilgrim people on their journeyings through the wilderness, but for a time it continued to be the centre for the corporate service of the nation when the land was possessed.

Eventually the chequered experiences of Israel under the Judges led to the establishment of the monarchy, firstly under Saul and then under David. Just as the historical record in the book of Judges shows the great influence exerted by the godly leaders, so the history of the period of the monarchy reveals the importance of the lead given by the king on the throne in relation to the service of God associated with His house.

Preparations by David

In the early part of Solomon's reign a high water mark was reached in Israel's experience when a magnificent temple was built and dedicated in Jerusalem. Although Solomon was the builder, the vision of such a building had first filled the mind of David his father. David's desire to build a more permanent structure for the Ark pleased God greatly, but it was not according to the divine purpose that he should actually construct it. David, however, was not discouraged and

15

continued to prepare for the project by amassing the necessary materials. His ready submission to the will of God, although it meant that he would not see his cherished desire fulfilled, was very commendable and is worthy of emulation.

It is a fundamental principle clearly established in Scripture that God supplies the pattern for His house, but that men build it (see Exodus 25:40). Solomon, although endowed with unique wisdom, did not use his own ideas in the design and construction of the Temple; he conformed to the God given plan. The pattern, apparently in written form, was communicated to David by the Holy Spirit (1 Chronicles 28:12-19). That pattern incorporated the details of the ordering of the service of song that David had introduced at the commandment of the Lord through His prophets (2 Chronicles 29:25). God revealed that the Temple was to be built on the site formerly held by the Jebusites but captured by David early in his reign. Such considerations reveal to us the vital contributions David made to the fulfilment of his cherished desire. He selected Jerusalem as his capital, and then later moved the Ark of God there, before the precise site that God had chosen for His dwelling-place had been revealed to him; this further shows how closely he was in tune with the purposes of God.

David's Vision Fulfilled

David's military prowess and his competent administration laid the foundation for the peace and prosperity enjoyed by Israel in the halcyon days of Solomon's reign. Solomon "in all his glory" provides us with a delightful foreshadowing of the millennial glory of Christ. The land possessed or controlled by Israel reached its maximum extent in Solomon's day. He "ruled over all the kingdoms from the River unto the land of the Philistines, and unto the border of Egypt: they brought presents, and served Solomon all the days of his life" (1 Kings 4:21). He had, "peace on all sides round about him. And Judah and Israel dwelt safely, every man under his vine and under his fig tree, from Dan even to Beersheba, all the days of Solomon" (1 Kings 4:24,25). It was this man of peace whom God chose to build the Temple in Jerusalem (1 Chronicles 22:9,10; 1 Kings 5:5) and provide us with a further analogy of millennial times (see Zechariah 6:12,13).

As Israel was strategically placed to control the major north-south caravan routes, Solomon derived an enormous revenue from the trade passing through his land. His alliance with Hiram, the king of Tyre, enabled him to exploit the sea routes also. So, "Solomon exceeded all the kings of the earth in riches and in wisdom. And all the earth sought the presence of Solomon, to hear his wisdom, which God had put in his heart" (1 Kings 10:23,24). These verses describe that golden age in Israel's history that was enjoyed during the reign of Solomon. The outstanding achievement of that remarkable reign was the completion and dedication of the Temple in Jerusalem. The inspired books of Proverbs, Ecclesiastes and Song of Songs are productions of that golden age, and from these we derive much instruction.

Will God dwell on the earth?

The building of the Temple took some seven years, and when it was completed the Ark of the Covenant was brought from the Tent that David had pitched for it in Jerusalem, and placed in the most holy place of the Temple. The separate services at Gibeon and at Jerusalem then ceased, and the new unified service in association with the Temple began. Then a visible seal of divine approval was given for, "when the priests were come out of the holy place ... the cloud filled the house of the LORD, so that the priests could not stand to minister by reason of the cloud: for the glory of the LORD filled the house of the LORD" (1 Kings 8:10,11; cf. Exodus 40:34,35). As Moses had faithfully complied with the pattern given to him for the Tabernacle, Solomon likewise strictly followed the specification of the Temple given to him. Even so, it was a cause of wonderment to Solomon that the great God of heaven should condescend to dwell in the Temple that he had built (1 Kings 8:27).

The vast concourse of Israel, assembled for the inauguration of the Temple services, witnessed a further unforgettable sight for, "when Solomon had made an end of praying, the fire came down from heaven, and consumed the burnt offering and the sacrifices; and the glory of the LORD filled the house" (2 Chronicles 7:1).

It should be noted that the dedication of the Temple took place in the seventh month; all Israel being assembled from the eighth day until the twenty-third day of that month (2 Chronicles 7:8-10). This period would embrace the day of Atonement (the tenth day) and the feast of Tabernacles (fifteenth to twenty-second day). It was essential that priest, people and sanctuary be cleansed by sacrifice for acceptable service (Hebrews 9:22-25), a cleansing that had to be repeated year by year.

Declension

After the dedication of the Temple God appeared again to Solomon and confirmed that He had hallowed the Temple and would not choose another earthly centre. He did, however, make it plain to Solomon that serious apostasy on the part of Israel would result in the Temple being forsaken by Him (1 Kings 9:6,7). The existence of a house for God depends upon the continuing obedience of God's people.

Israel reached the zenith of her national glory in the early part of Solomon's reign because of the commendable attitude of the king: "Solomon loved the LORD, walking in the statutes of David his father" (1 Kings 3:3). His request for an "understanding heart" so pleased God that he was given other blessings that he had not asked for (1 Kings 3:9-13). In making this request he had evidently been influenced by the instruction given him by his father (Proverbs 4:3-5). It is with sadness, however, that we note that he did not maintain fidelity throughout his reign. In his old age "his wives turned away his heart after other gods" (1 Kings 11:4). His great wisdom did not keep him faithful, for he failed to take his own advice "keep thy heart with all diligence" (Proverbs 4:23).

A Spiritual House

God does not now dwell in a temple made with hands (Acts 7:48), but in a spiritual house composed of living stones (1 Peter 2:5). The pattern of the spiritual house is given in the apostles' teaching. The apostles received it from the Lord Himself; particularly during the post-resurrection period when he was with them during forty days "speaking the things concerning the kingdom of God" (Acts 1:3). In this there is a parallel with the transmission of the pattern of the Tabernacle to Moses (Exodus 24:18). The apostles, like Moses and like Solomon, faithfully put the transmitted pattern into practice and they too witnessed a dramatic indication of divine approval for "there appeared unto them tongues parting asunder, like as of fire; and it sat upon each one of them" (Acts 2:3). The Holy Spirit had come down to indwell men and to take up His dwelling in the spiritual house that initially was formed by one hundred and twenty "living stones" (Acts 1:15; 2:1 4; cf. Leviticus 9:24; 2 Chronicles 7:1).

The provisos that applied to the material house in Solomon's day apply to the spiritual house in our day. Its continuing existence depends upon continuing obedience on the part of the people of God. This point is well made by the writer to the Hebrews: "whose house are we, if we hold fast our boldness and the glorying of our hope firm unto the end" (Hebrews 3:6).

Millennial Foreshadowing

The glory of Solomon's reign provides us with many parallels to that future glorious day when David's greater Son will reign with world-wide authority, and it is evident that God intended this to be so. Solomon's work in building the Temple illustrates the fulfilment of the prophecy of Zechariah 6:12,13. A magnificent temple will be built in Jerusalem by the Lord, most probably according to the pattern given in the book of Ezekiel, and it will become the centre for the worship of all the nations of the earth (Isaiah 2:2,3). The unique wisdom of Solomon, as exemplified in the judgement he gave in the incident related in 1 Kings 3:16-28, foreshadows the perfect, righteous judgements of the "greater than Solomon".

When He reigns, "He shall not judge after the sight of His eyes, neither reprove after the hearing of His ears: but with righteousness ... and with equity ..." (Isaiah 11.3,4), for He is able to "bring to light the hidden things of darkness, and make manifest the counsels of the hearts" (1 Corinthians 4:5). The peace and prosperity that will characterize the millennial age is beautifully described in Psalm 72:7,8, a psalm fittingly ascribed to Solomon. Creation too will rejoice and know a liberation when the Creator reigns in that future golden age.

"All shall be well in His kingdom of peace, Freedom shall flourish and wisdom increase; Foe shall be friend when His triumph we sing, Sword shall be sickle when Jesus is King".

CHAPTER FOUR: VICTORY AND CLEANSING UNDER ASA

"THAT WHICH WAS GOOD and right"

Some fifty years before Asa received the kingdom, King Solomon prayed in the court of the newly glorified Temple that the Lord would hear "the stranger, that is not of Thy people Israel, when he shall come out of a far country for Thy name's sake ... and pray toward this house". Visitors and immigrants would be drawn by the report of Jehovah's great name and mighty hand and stretched out arm, how nation after nation was subdued before Israel, and how David and his captains established possession of the land. Surely Solomon, with the wise and understanding heart of his prime, also saw that victory had been granted so that the iniquities of the Amorite might give place to a way of life that God could bless.

The first verses of Numbers 25 and the warnings of Leviticus 18 show how any respect for the Canaanites' religion and festivals led on to the basest of selfish pleasures and even the cruellest human sacrifice (Leviticus 18:21, 2 Kings 3:27). Yet by the reign of Solomon's son, favoured Judah, with God's centre in their capital, had returned to idol-worship. They "built them high places, and pillars, and Asherim, on every high hill and under every green tree; and there were also sodomites in the land: they did according to all the abominations of the nations which the LORD drove out" (1 Kings 14:23,24). There was also no peace for Judah under Rehoboam (14:25-30). The three year reign of Abijah followed, and though he and his army are commended in 2 Chronicles 13 for their reliance upon the Lord when ambushed by Israel, yet "he walked in all the sins of his father". His son Asa received the throne only because God had promised it to David's line. All the more striking is the Chronicler's first comment on Asa's rule: "In his days the land was quiet ten years."

What brought such security? It did not come because Abijah had captured border cities from Israel - including Bethel with the golden calf. Nor was peace established by leaving the people undisturbed in the ways they had chosen. We are told that Asa "had no war in those years; because the LORD had given him rest". Surely rest was granted because Asa first chose to do what was good and right, and then took vigorous action. He organized the destruction of altar, image, hill-shrine and Asherah-pole, and sent out the royal command to seek the Lord and do the law. Even after such rigorous intervention in highly sensitive matters, "the kingdom was quiet before him". We are reminded of James' instruction for saints involved in "wars" and "fightings": "Be subject therefore unto God; but resist the devil, and he will flee from you. Draw nigh to God, and He will draw nigh to you".

Rest and Prosperity

So the king and the nation built and prospered. That is to say, the years of rest were filled with constructive activity. Walled cities were built to ensure lasting security in which to recover the divine pattern of national life, with its remarkable provision for the poor, the debtor, the manslayer, the settler and the distinct achievement of each tribe. Now, securing possession of the national inheritance is described in Hebrews 4. Though the task had been begun under Joshua's leadership, the Spirit urged in Psalm 95 that it be continued, "saying in David, after so long a time.

Today if ye shall hear his voice, Harden not your hearts".

The writer to the Hebrews then argues that in our era also "There remaineth therefore a sabbath rest for the people of God" and, he says, to enter into that rest demands diligence. Here is our lesson from Asa's building projects. The walls and towers, gates and bars are for us, we suggest, the ability of each saint to witness to the truths of God's kingdom by word and by deed. To hold fast the glorying of our hope entails being separated from unbelievers to the service of God. Then we will be able both to live as partakers of the divine nature should, and to appeal to others, that they may also taste that the Lord is gracious.

Revival is the recovery of this power, and Peter describes how it can be achieved. In opening his second letter he starts with a fresh appreciation of the promises of God, and how we have been cleansed from our old sins. He calls for "all diligence" that we may be "not idle nor unfruitful unto the knowledge of our Lord Jesus Christ". We note also that spiritual life includes patience and knowledge (2 Peter 1:4-8). There is something of this in the instruction in Psalm 46, "Be still, and know that I am God". Let us pray that in our time we shall have many like Asa who will direct and encourage our building,

Victory and Covenant

Then came a host of the sons of Ham to Mareshah, which was one of the cities assigned to the tribe of Judah, and means 'Possession'. Asa had increased his army to 180,000 more than his father mustered against Jeroboam. But again the enemy had an army twice as large, and chariots besides. Again, however, the men of Judah cried to the Lord; and the king led their prayer. "So the LORD smote the Ethiopians before Asa, and before Judah; and the Ethiopians fled". Then it is we read of the Spirit of God coming upon the prophet: after conflict, encouragement and warning was sent. We may ask ourselves if, when we think our service has been successful, we remember to turn to the Lord for His assessment, and wait upon Him to know what should follow victory.

So Asa took courage "and put away the abominations ..." We might expect such things in the cities which he had taken from the hill-country of Ephraim. But the task had also to be done in "all the land of Judah and Benjamin". Probably only ten years, or fifteen at most, after the first great cleansing, but long enough for the journeys to Jerusalem to become irksome, for the teaching priest to find competition from the local shrines. Long enough for self-advancement to fill the heart, and covetousness, which is idolatry, to take control.

Azariah had addressed all Judah and Benjamin as well as the king: "your work" reminds us that cleansing was not the responsibility only of the king's officers, the priests and the Levites. The record of the great gathering at Jerusalem that entered into covenant to seek the Lord repeats the word "they" in verse after verse, for "all Judah rejoiced at the oath". As

Deborah and Barak sang, "For that the leaders took the lead in Israel, For that the people offered themselves willingly, Bless ye the LORD" (Judges 5:1,2)

"But the high places were not taken away out of Israel"

In spite of the removal of the high places at the beginning of the reign, and the purging of "the abominations" after Azariah's prophecy, the final summary still has to be that the high places were not taken away out of Israel. 1 Kings 15:14 shows that in 2 Chronicles 15:17 "Israel" does refer to the Southern kingdom. At the end of the reigns of Jehoshophat, Joash, Amaziah, and Uzziah, it again has to be recorded that the shrines on the high places were still reverenced.

Why were they so stubborn a problem? Doubtless to us also the tops of the numerous lower hills of Judah, in country or suburb, would have seemed ideal settings for worship. They were free from interruption, set apart by a little effort taken in going there, suggesting ascent from earth to heaven, and attractive to every other race that had occupied the land. For a deeper experience, one could climb even the high mountains (Deuteronomy 12:2). Why not sanctify them to the service of Jehovah? There would be many that still had foundations of old shrines that could be built again to make the privacy complete. So man might reason if left to himself.

But praise the God of heaven and earth for the richness and rightness of His design. For the twelve tribes whom He had delivered from Egypt there was to be one centre for service. The purpose is set out for us to consider: "that thou mayest learn to fear the LORD thy God always". From the chosen place the priests and Levites who had completed their courses of duty returned to their homes, dispersed by divine appointment among the tribes' inheritances (1 Chronicles 6:54, ff.). Their teaching of the law would be informed by the glories of the Temple service, and their experience of men of every walk of life coming in repentance or in thanksgiving. How could any withdrawal to the high places and the rituals that gathered round them compare with the pilgrimage that, passing through the valley, made it a place of springs, or the throng going to the house of God, with the voice of joy and praise?

Covenant with Syria

From the time of Judah's covenant to seek the Lord till the thirty-fifth year of Asa's reign there was no more war. Then the old ambition in the north arose again, and Baasha built Ramah in order to control the border-traffic. Asa's response in his closing years makes sad reading, each detail spelling out the failure of faith in a man whose heart was accounted "perfect all his days".

The first action described in both 1 Kings 15 and 2 Chronicles 16 was to bring out silver and gold out of the treasures of the house of the Lord and of the king's house. Why dedicate treasures to the Lord (2 Chronicles 15:18) if in the end they were to be used to buy help from an enemy of Israel, instead of waiting on the Lord? There is no mention of the covenant of Asa's fifteenth year, through which Judah was granted abiding rest. Instead, a covenant with the king of Syria is proposed, and the idea supported by talk of a former league between the kings' fathers that we do not read of elsewhere. And was there no security in the fortified cities built in the first ten years of quiet? The policy brought apparent success, but divine rebuke and the promise of coming wars. The king then imprisoned the prophet, and oppressed some of the people, for as his fear of the Lord declined, so did wisdom in government. And at the last, when he became severely diseased in his feet, Asa "sought not unto the LORD, but to the physicians".

Building for Eternity

Seeing the disappointment of those final years, we may ask which of Asa's works had lasting effect. We leave with God the assessment of what, in Asa's life and in ours abides for eternity. But certain legacies of the 41-year long reign can be plainly traced in Old Testament history. When the finest of Judah had been taken into captivity, Ishmael, an officer of the seed royal, conspired against the governor appointed by Nebuchadnezzar, and then slew seventy men from Israel who were on their way to Jerusalem with offerings. He filled a pit in Mizpah with the slain; and the pit was "that which Asa the king had made for fear of Baasha" (Jeremiah 41:9).

But that reminder of failure is outweighed by the effect of Asa's godly example, through thirty-five years, that inspired his son Jehoshaphat to lead Judah again in seeking the Lord.

CHAPTER FIVE: JEHOSHAPHAT – REFORMER AND CONQUEROR

———

THE TWENTY-FIVE YEARS of the reign of Jehoshaphat were among the most notable in all the history of the people of Judah. For much of this period, material prosperity and military supremacy were enjoyed. Yet within it there were times of spiritual declension, when Jehoshaphat led his people contrary to the will of God. His reign provides a clear example of the principle that revival among the people of God frequently results from faithfulness on the part of the leaders - allied, of course, to the willingness of the people to receive instruction and follow good example.

Early spiritual condition

The early days of Jehoshaphat's reign were clearly times of great spiritual resolve. To the casual reader, the introductory statement that he "strengthened himself against Israel" is, perhaps, surprising, but it must be remembered that, in the closing years of Asa, his father, Israel had set herself up as Judah's implacable enemy (16:1). It was in defence, therefore, of the safety of his people against the incursions of an apostate Israel that Jehoshaphat placed strategic garrisons throughout the land.

In these early days the spiritual integrity of Jehoshaphat was of a high order. One is moved to admiration by the divine commendation of the young king. "He walked in the first ways of his father David ... sought to the God of his father, and walked in His commandments ... his heart was lifted up in the ways of the Lord". The word and will of Jehovah occupied the prime place in his life. This is the hallmark of the true man of God, and it is only through men with sanctified and submissive wills that God can work. Jehoshaphat's leadership in loyalty to the will of God led his people back to the purity and truth of the worship of the Lord.

A teaching ministry

Not only did Jehoshaphat devote himself to keeping the law of his God, but he also organized its teaching among the people. Three years into his reign, Jehoshaphat "sent his princes ... to teach in the cities of Judah; and with them the Levites ... and ... the priests. And they taught in Judah, having the book of the law of the Lord with them" The spiritual lives of the people of God can only be nourished by feeding on His word, and regulated by its observance. Failure in this leads, inevitably, to spiritual weakness. It is one of the prime functions of leaders among God's people to teach "the doctrine which is according to godliness" (1 Timothy 6:3). In their day, the apostles were keenly aware of the importance of a right understanding of the word of God by the people of God. We remember, for example, that Paul made it a matter of constant prayer that the Colossian disciples would be "filled with the knowledge of His will in all spiritual wisdom and understanding, to walk worthily of the Lord unto all pleasing" (Colossians 1:9,10).

It is instructive to note that, in Jehoshaphat's case, the exercise to teach others followed his own practical obedience to the word. This is a godly principle which, among others, was later seen in Ezra, who "had set his heart to seek the law of the LORD, and to do it, and to teach in Israel statutes and judgements" (Ezra 7:10).

"It shall be well with them that fear God, which fear before Him" (Ecclesiastes 8:12), and Jehoshaphat and his kingdom proved that the blessing of the Lord is upon those who are obedient to His word. The surrounding nations "made no war against Jehoshaphat". The king himself increased in greatness, and his military prowess was considerable. He also "had riches and honour in abundance". The lesson that obedience to the revealed will of God is the path to blessing is writ large on the page of Scripture, yet how slow we are to learn it. "To obey is better than sacrifice", is a message as valid today as when spoken to the unhappy Saul at Gilgal (1 Samuel 15:22).

Separation surrendered

With an apparently startling suddenness, Jehoshaphat made affinity with the king of Israel. When one takes into account Israel's departure from God, alliance with her could not be other than wrong, and the wrong was compounded by the character of the man who was Israel's king, for Ahab "did sell himself to do that which was evil in the sight of the LORD" (1 Kings 21:25). The early verses of 2 Chronicles 18 indicate strongly that Jehoshaphat had entered into this liaison without seeking the mind of the Lord. Had he done so, this disastrous alliance would never have taken place.

The propensity for self-will is strong in all of us, and Jehoshaphat evinced it right to the end of this unhappy episode in his life. True, he insisted on hearing what Micaiah the prophet had to say, but despite the clarity of the warning given, "the king of Israel and Jehoshaphat the king of Judah went up to Ramoth-gilead". Jehoshaphat's experience provides but one example of the disastrous consequences of following our own will. "Thy word is a lamp unto my feet, and light unto my path" (Psalm 119:105), is the only guideline for us to follow. Failure to observe the will of God, as revealed to us in His word, will end in spiritual tragedy.

For Jehoshaphat, that end was only narrowly averted. In battle against the Syrians, he was mistaken for the king of Israel, and came under severe attack. But "Jehoshaphat cried out, and the LORD helped him". "If we are faithless, He abideth faithful" (2 Timothy 2:13). A merciful God intervened to save the life of His faithless servant.

For Jehoshaphat, there was a solemn lesson to be learned from this experience. On his return in peace to Jerusalem, he was met by Jehu the son of Hanani the seer, who, among other things, informed him that, "For this thing wrath is upon thee from the LORD". The principle that, "whatsoever a man soweth, that shall he also reap" (Galatians 6:7) applies to the people of God in every day. Jehoshaphat's ungodly liaison with Ahab had tragic results both for his nation and for his immediate family. Jehoram, his son, married Ahab's daughter, murdered his own brothers, and died of incurable disease "without being desired". All of Jehoram's sons, except the youngest, were slain at the hands of the Arabians (22:1), and all the seed royal (save Joash, who had been hidden away) were put to death by Jehoram's evil widow, Athaliah. May the Lord keep His people of this generation loyal to the carrying out of His revealed will!

Happily, Jehoshaphat found repentance, and 2 Chronicles 19 is a record of revival in the true sense of that word. The rebuke by Jehu appears to have been taken to heart, and once more Jehoshaphat applied himself to the doing of the will of God.

He "dwelt at Jerusalem" - the place in which God had chosen to place His name. Jerusalem, "the city of the great king", occupied a unique place in the dealings of God with His people. It was the place of His testimony and of His service, and He rejoiced to see His people there. The lead given by Jehoshaphat to his people in this matter was one of vital significance. Similarly, in contrast to the sad leadership he gave in chapter 18, Jehoshaphat now showed the true characteristics of a leader among God's people, in that, "he went out again among the people ... and brought them back unto the Lord, the God of their fathers".

This was the period, too, in which Jehoshaphat set judges throughout all the fenced cities of Judah. Rule among the people of God is an indispensable part of their divine constitution. David had written of Jerusalem, "There are set thrones for judgement" (Psalm 122:5), and the spiritual welfare of God's people is dependent on, among other things, the administration of His rule. Jehoshaphat's charge to the judges (19:6-11) is worth consideration. Faithfulness in judgement is vital. Courage in its administration is needed. No respect of persons must be shown. Judgement must be executed in the fear of the Lord. And the people must constantly be warned, "that they be not guilty toward the LORD". The application of all this to God's New Covenant people is clear. But, for its perfect outworking we must look to the coming One, of whom it is written, "His delight shall be in the fear of the LORD: and He shall not judge after the sight of His eyes, neither reprove after the hearing of His ears: but with righteousness shall He judge the poor, and reprove with equity for the meek of the earth" (Isaiah 11:3,4).

Relying on God

It has been part of the experience of the people of God in every age to come under attack, and Jehoshaphat's day was no exception. Against him there came "a great multitude" of his enemies. The danger could not be ignored. The defence of the nation was imperative - but their best (and only) defence lay in the Lord. Jehoshaphat exemplified the spirit expressed by the writer of Psalm 121, "I will lift up mine eyes unto the mountains: from whence shall my help come? My help cometh from the LORD, which made heaven and earth". Thus, when human counsel would have been to take up arms, Jehoshaphat "set himself to seek unto the Lord". Once again, his leadership of the people in a matter of vital importance had the desired result, for "Judah gathered themselves together, to seek help of the LORD: even out of all the cities of Judah they came to seek the Lord". "Call upon Me in the day of trouble; I will deliver thee, and thou shalt glorify Me", is the promise of God (Psalm 50:15), a promise the truth of which Judah was about to discover.

The trust and dependence shown by Jehoshaphat and Judah was dramatically honoured by the Lord. Through Jahaziel, the Spirit of God brought assurance to their troubled hearts. "Fear not, neither be dismayed ... Ye shall not need to fight in this battle". Perhaps most startling of all was the repetition of the word given to their forefathers when, on leaving Egypt, they found themselves trapped between the Red Sea and the pursuing army, "Stand ye still, and see the salvation of the Lord with you" (20:17; cf. Exodus 14:13). What God promised, He performed in the most wonderful way. We shall pass over the story of how He effected their deliverance, but note that the people whose faith in the Lord's promise was demonstrated by their praise and singing as they went out to meet the foe, returned after the victory to the house of God, "with psalteries and harps and trumpets".

The prosperity and tranquility which followed this experience were remarkable. The presence of God among His people and His intervention against their enemies became widely known, "so the realm of Jehoshaphat was quiet: for his God gave him rest round about". Isn't the lesson clear? Separation to the Lord, loyalty to His word, trust in His power to keep and deliver, and faithful service in His house are all necessary if His people are to know divine power and blessing. When, like Jehoshaphat, we conform to these principles of personal and collective service, we shall know the presence of the Lord among us, with all the promise of revival which this implies.

Sadly, the history of Jehoshaphat does not stop at this point. Over all, his record was good, "doing that which was right in the eyes of the Lord", but the end of his life was once more marred by departure. It was the old problem re-appearing, Again, he made affinity with a king of Israel, one who "did very wickedly".

And once again the episode ended in disaster. "Because thou hast joined thyself with Ahaziah", he was told, "The Lord hath destroyed thy works".

Surely, in the record of the life of Jehoshaphat, the Spirit of God is laying particular emphasis on the immense importance of separation in the lives of the people of God. Principles of divine gathering must be safeguarded and the dangers of wrong associations avoided. "Come ye out from among them, and be ye separate" (2 Corinthians 6:17), is a divine command whose observance today, as in the days of the early churches, will bring blessing to the people of God.

CHAPTER SIX: A VETERAN PRIEST AND A BOY KING

———

THIS EPISODE OF REVIVAL is recorded in 2 Kings 11:1-12:21; 2 Chronicles 22:1-24:27.

Crisis

Joash was the sole survivor of a brutal family massacre. This foul crime was the work of his grandmother, Athalia, described in Scripture as "that wicked woman". Such an outright condemnation of a woman is not found elsewhere in the Bible. She was the daughter of king Ahab of Israel and his wife Jezebel, the Zidonian Baal-worshipper. As part of a disastrous political alliance between Israel and Judah, Athalia had been married to Jehoshaphat's son, Jehoram. Sadly, good king Jehoshaphat had put political expediency before the necessity for separation from evil. This grave error in an otherwise successful reign brought the royal line through Solomon very near to extinction.

After Jehoram died, Athalia's son, king Ahaziah, was killed by Jehu in the execution of divine judgement on the wicked house of Ahab. But the bereaved mother, instead of mourning her loss, saw in it the opportunity to satisfy her lust for power and usurp rule over the kingdom of Judah. Without scruple she proceeded to murder her own grandchildren, the remaining heirs to the throne. But a princess, who was the wife of Jehoiada the High

Priest, became aware of what was being done. She managed to rescue the youngest prince, baby Joash, and hide him in the Temple.

We do not know whether Athalia was aware of the survival of an heir to the throne, but we are told that she "reigned over the land". This unusual phrase seems to suggest that although there was no one powerful enough to question her right to rule, there was some limitation to her authority. For instance, it is obvious from subsequent events that she had little say about what went on within the Temple precincts. Other rulers of Judah had exercised authority over the house of God, sometimes for good and sometimes for ill, but Athalia was no match for Jehoiada, a man of great faith and determination. His wife too must have been a woman of singular faith and courage to have rescued the baby prince from under the nose of the imperious Athalia.

King's daughter and High Priest were fine examples of two who were "joint-heirs of the grace of life" and "fellow-workers unto the kingdom of God", examples which we do well to emulate. In a critical and dangerous time for the people of God, they together trained the child in the fear of God for future kingship. They carefully planned for the great day when Joash would sit on the throne as the rightful king of Judah. It was a responsible task, for much was at stake. Would the royal line survive? Would Athalia frustrate their plans and extend her authority to prevent the worship of God in His house? No doubt they were much cast upon God, trusting His promise, "that David My servant may have a lamp always before Me in Jerusalem, the city which I have chosen Me to put My Name there" (1 Kings 11:36). In perilous times this godly couple had the welfare of the house of God and the kingdom of God at heart. As a consequence God richly blessed them, and He will do the same today for those who, in similarly difficult times, have the same care for the things of God.

Deliverance

When Joash was seven years old Jehoiada judged that the time had come for Athalia's usurpation to be brought to an end. He made a careful assessment of the help he could count on from priests, Levites and soldiers. On a set day he mustered all these loyal subjects in the Temple precincts and gave them weapons. He directed operations with precision and skill. When all was prepared, Joash was brought out, surrounded by a heavy guard. Could this little boy survive in such adverse circumstances? Surely yes, because the Lord was on his side, and moreover, the continuation of the Messianic line depended on his preservation.

Amid great rejoicing the royal crown was placed on the king's head and Jehoiada anointed him king of Judah as he symbolically held the Law of God in his hand. Then all the people clapped their hands and shouted "God save the king". From the palace Athalia heard the noise and came to investigate. When she saw the king with the crown on his head she shouted, "Treason, treason" (strange accusation from a woman with such an evil record!) She was powerless in the face of the vast array of armed men, and on the High Priest's instructions she was put to death as soon as she left the Temple courts.

Jehoiada's next step was to see that the king and all the people joined him in covenanting that they would be the Lord's people. Then they all went to the house of Baal and destroyed both it and its priest. Finally the services of God's house which were divinely instituted through David, were recommenced.

Restoration

When Joash reached mature years he was active in restoring the Temple, which had been badly damaged by the Baal-worshipping sons of Athalia. The people gladly and generously contributed to the cost and the workmen went to work with a will. It was a heavy task, but it was eventually completed and vessels of gold and silver for the services were made with the gifts left over. It was now possible for the burnt offerings to be offered continually as required by the law of Moses.

The inspired historian writes that these offerings were made "all the days of Jehoiada" ominous hint of what was to come! The High Priest died at the great age of 130 years; "he had done good in Israel, and toward God and His house". This was the commendation of Scripture; furthermore, although not of the royal line, he was buried in the city of David among the kings. No greater honour could have been given to him than this unique burial. He left a tremendous example for all disciples of the Lord Jesus Christ to follow.

It is recorded that "Joash did that which was right in the eyes of the LORD all the days of Jehoiada the priest"; but after the old man died it became apparent that he alone had been the driving force in all the reforms of Joash's reign. The king seems to have been genuinely inspired by the enthusiasm of his guardian for the house of God. But he was a man who could easily be led, so that when the princes of Judah assumed their traditional role as advisers to the king, the results were disastrous.

Declension

With the connivance of the king, Judah once again lapsed into idolatry. The people forsook God's house, thereby bringing the wrath of God upon the kingdom, and they refused to listen to the prophets whom God sent to warn them. At last Jehoiada's son, with the same faithfulness and courage which characterized his father, remonstrated in public with the men of Judah: 'Why transgress ye the commandments of the LORD, that ye cannot prosper? Because ye have forsaken the LORD, He hath forsaken you". Far from heeding the rebuke, they stoned him to death in the court of the house of the Lord. This foul deed was instigated by the king himself; "thus Joash the king remembered not the kindness which Jehoiada ... had done to him."

Divine retribution came shortly afterwards. A small company of Syrians "destroyed all the princes of the people ... and sent all the spoil of them unto the king of Damascus". Joash was left severely wounded (see Revised Standard Version) and became the victim of a conspiracy in his own household. In revenge for the death of Jehoiada's son, his servants killed him in bed.

In contrast to the high honour given to Jehoiada in his death, Joash was denied what might have been considered the right of a king of Judah to be buried with David in the tombs of the kings. So ended a long reign of forty years which began with such promise. The great achievements of earlier life were overshadowed by later failures. It is regrettably possible for a Christian life to end like that. However good the beginning, nothing can outweigh unfaithfulness in later life. May we aim to imitate the apostle Paul who, when death approached, said, "I have finished the course, I have kept the faith", consequently God had a crown ready for him (2 Timothy 4:7,8).

The principal cause of Joash's downfall seems to have been that he placed too much reliance upon others and had little personal conviction. We are thankful for the support and instruction of faithful men of God, but a lesson we can learn from the life of Joash is that it is necessary to be assured in our own minds of the truth of God. We need to become "full-grown men" and attain "the measure of the stature of the fulness of Christ: that we may be no longer children, tossed to and fro with every wind of doctrine, by the sleight of men, in craftiness, after the wiles of error; but ... may grow up in all things into Him, which is the Head, even Christ" (Ephesians 4:13-15).

CHAPTER SEVEN: HEZEKIAH'S FAITHFULNESS AND OVERCOMING FAITH

———

TO RULE AND GOVERN a nation is a heavy responsibility calling for special abilities and qualities which are given to few. The consequences of failure are serious. When the divine trust to rule in righteousness is betrayed and a nation is led into idolatry and rebellion, the judgement of God is inevitable. Divine judgement falls upon the people and the ruler alike.

The histories of the kingdoms of Israel and Judah are marred by the disobedience of several kings who led their subjects away from God. Others, being God-fearing men, led their people back to the right paths, restored the spiritual life of the nation, and established again the true worship of Jehovah.

The divine record indicates that the state of the nation was almost always directly related to the attitude of the reigning king towards the law of the Lord and to the house of God. We read of example after example where the people followed the lead of their monarch, for good or for evil.

Hezekiah is an outstanding example of a king who was faithful to the divine trust and of whom it is said, "He did that which was right in the eyes of the LORD" (2 Kings 18:3).

At the age of twenty-five he succeeded to the throne of Judah after the death of his idolatrous father. He inherited a kingdom which was in a poor condition spiritually and in a perilous situation politically. He reigned for 29 years, during which time he not only brought about spiritual and religious reforms, but also displayed faith and courage in the international politics of his day.

Isaiah the prophet, who had been speaking the word of the Lord to Judah from the days of Uzziah and through the reigns of Jotham and Ahaz, was still active when Hezekiah came to the throne. While the prophet's ministry was apparently having little effect upon Ahaz, his first son Hezekiah was made of different stuff and the words of Isaiah were quietly preparing the young prince for the day when the sceptre would be in his hands. He proved to be a spiritually-minded young man who was faithful to the word of the Lord.

At the beginning of his reign Hezekiah cleansed the Temple from defilement and restored the service of the house of God (see 2 Chronicles 29). It required sixteen days to clean up the filth with which the Temple had been polluted. He restored the worship of Jehovah, offering sin-offerings, burnt offerings and peace offerings. Singing and music were again heard in the courts of the Lord's house. His spiritual sensitivity is seen in his concern for those still remaining in the northern kingdom, for he sent his posts round the towns and villages inviting the people to come to worship the Lord in Jerusalem.

The Passover was also reinstituted, although with some ritual deviations. It was recommenced on the fourteenth day of the second month and not of the first month. Some who took part in the Passover were ceremonially unclean; Hezekiah obviously being of the mind that the spirit was more important than the letter on such a great occasion of reformation. The Feast of Unleavened Bread which followed the Passover was prolonged to fourteen days (twice as long as the statutory period) by popular consent, so great was the fervour of this national revival. The priesthood in its courses was reinstated and the service of the Levites recommenced. Tithing was again introduced to maintain the service of the house and the priesthood. The high places with their unclean altars and images were destroyed not only in Judah but in the northern kingdom also.

Hezekiah shines out from the darkness of his day as one who loved the Lord and His Word. He knew that the only hope for the nation was for the people to return to the Lord and serve Him in His house. His aim was to restore the spiritual life of his subjects by a return to the great festivals of Jehovah and to the practical application of the Law in their daily lives as individuals. When all this work of recommencing the service of God was finished it is said of Hezekiah, "And thus did Hezekiah throughout all Judah; and he wrought that which was good and right and faithful before the LORD his God. And in every work that he began in the service of the house of God, and in the law, and in the commandments, to seek his God, he did it with all his heart, and prospered" (2 Chronicles 31:20,21).

Hezekiah was, however, not just a great spiritual reformer and religious leader. He was also a practical engineer and a shrewd politician. His public works can still be seen in Jerusalem today. He appreciated the strategic importance of water to Jerusalem should the city ever be besieged, and the advantage to the defenders of denying water to the besieging army. He diverted the spring of Gihon (2 Chronicles 32:30) into the city by cutting water tunnels through the solid rock, bringing the water into the Pool of Siloam, one of the city's reservoirs.

He reigned in a period of political instability. The divided kingdoms of Israel and Judah were political pawns in the game being played by the great powers of Assyria and Egypt. Although only pawns, nevertheless they could not be ignored because of their important geographical position astride the main routes north and south. Hezekiah inherited from his father the condition of being tributary to Assyria, and Isaiah seemed not to favour breaking this obligation. Perhaps the recent overthrow of Samaria by Assyria had been a solemn reminder of the consequences of offending such a powerful nation. Isaiah advised against any alliance with Egypt against Assyria (Isaiah 30:1-3; 7-15). However, Hezekiah rebelled, and the inevitable happened. Assyria took action against the kingdom of Judah and attacked Jerusalem.

At a public meeting of the citizens of Jerusalem Hezekiah rallied their support to his proposed resistance to Sennacherib. The might of Assyria did not frighten him when he knew that God was with him. He said to the people "for there is a greater with us than with him. With him is an arm of flesh; but with us is the

LORD our God to help us, to fight our battles" (2 Chronicles 32:7-8). And the people "rested themselves upon the words of Hezekiah" (2 Chronicles 32:8).

Sennacherib eventually came to Jerusalem and surrounded the city. A remarkable attempt at psychological warfare then took place when the Assyrians tried to influence the defenders of the city by skillful propaganda. Their attempt to counter the effect of Hezekiah's five words shows that their military intelligence had been good. By the spoken and written word they belittled the power of Jehovah to save Jerusalem, pointing out that in other places the gods of the people were helpless in the defence of their worshippers. They ridiculed an alliance with Egypt as being powerless to stop Assyria.

Try as they would, however, their threats could not shake the people who had been strengthened by the personal faith and courage of Hezekiah. This is all the more remarkable in that those in Jerusalem knew the power and destructive potential of the Assyrian army. It was evident just by looking over the city wall that the odds against them were overwhelming, Yet they were prepared to follow Hezekiah's leadership. Like David his forefather, who accepted Goliath the Philistine's challenge to the God of Israel, Hezekiah heard this new challenge to Jehovah by the heathen Assyrians and was not prepared to let it go unanswered. He took the matter to the Lord. The honour of the God of Israel was at stake. Hezekiah never doubted the ability of Jehovah to deliver the city, but perhaps he wondered whether the purposes of God for Judah were similar to that which had befallen the northern kingdom.

The answer to Hezekiah came through Isaiah. "I have heard thee" (2 Kings 19:20). The prophet then uttered God's judgement against Assyria (2 Kings 19:21-34) which had its dreadful fulfilment that very night. The purposes of God for His people were under His control and were not at the disposal of the Assyrians, or of any other nation.

"The zeal of the LORD shall perform this ... He (the Assyrian) shall not come unto this city ... By the way that he came ... he shall return ... For I will defend this city to save it, for Mine own sake, and for My servant David's sake" (2 Kings 19:31-34).

One of the most amazing events in the history of God's people then took place with the mysterious destruction of the Assyrian host and the evacuation of their encampment. Byron describes this in his famous poem "The Destruction of Sennacherib",

"For the angel of death spread his wings on the blast,

And breathed in the face of the foe as he passed. .

"And the might of the Gentile, unsmote by the sword,

Hath melted like snow in the glance of the Lord".

The destruction of the city and the captivity, of the people were thus delayed for some years, undoubtedly because of the faith of Hezekiah. Unfortunately it was only a postponement of the evil day. Idolatry and rebellion which would not yield entirely to the pleading of the prophets or the reforming zeal of the king required that in captivity and exile the people of God would learn the basic lesson that God would teach them, "Thou shalt have none other gods before Me" (Exodus 20:3).

Hezekiah's illness provided yet another example of his faith. He pleaded with the Lord for a lengthening of his life on the ground of his faithfulness in earlier years: "Remember now, O LORD, I beseech Thee, how I have walked before Thee in truth and with a perfect heart, and have done that which is good in Thy sight" (2 Kings 20:3).

Perhaps he also knew that after his death the kingdom would be overthrown and the city destroyed. His pleading therefore may not have been from selfish motives only, but also for the postponement of the judgement of the Lord upon his kingdom (see 2 Kings 20:6). His faith and his tears prevailed with his God and a further fifteen years were given to him, and also to the people. The remarkable sign which Hezekiah requested was given by the shadow returning on the dial of Ahaz by ten degrees. Again, his request for a sign may not have been purely selfish. The sign would have been public knowledge and is possibly the "wonder that was done in the land" (2 Chronicles 32:31) which the Babylonians sent men to investigate. The sign from the Lord to Hezekiah was a witness to his own kingdom and to other nations also.

At this point it would seem that his faith wavered again. He should have glorified God by testifying to the visiting ambassadors about the goodness of the Lord in lengthening his years, but rather he gloried in the display of his treasures. This gave Isaiah the occasion to speak the word of the Lord to him (Isaiah 39:5-7), and to foretell the carrying away to Babylon of his family and the spoiling of his possessions. Once more, however, the underlying faith of the man is seen in his acceptance of the word of the prophet. He said to Isaiah, "Good is the word of the LORD which thou hast spoken" (Isaiah 39:8). Hezekiah's determination to live out his days in righteousness is also seen in what may well have been his last recorded words, "For there shall be peace and truth in my days" (Isaiah 39:8).

CHAPTER EIGHT: JOSHUA'S SPIRITUAL LEADERSHIP

―――

HIS TIMES

Josiah became king of Judah in the seventh century before the birth of Christ. The first millennium of Israel's history as the people of God can be considered as two periods of about five centuries each. The first period extended from the Exodus to the time of David and Solomon, in the course of which Israel advanced from being a nation of slaves to the highest point of their national power and prosperity in the kingdom of Solomon. The second period of five centuries began with that time of spiritual and material greatness and concluded with the captivity of Judah and the spoiling of Jerusalem by king Nebuchadnezzar of Babylon.

This part of Israel's history saw a divided kingdom and can be regarded as a period of steady spiritual decline relieved only by brief times of revival under certain kings of Judah who "did … right in the eyes of the LORD, and walked in the ways of David". Josiah was one of these notable examples and he came to the throne of Judah near the end of the five hundred year period. Israel had already been carried captive to Assyria and after Josiah's death the passage of only a further twenty-two years saw the end of the kingdom of Judah in the Babylonian captivity.

The kings of Judah who immediately preceded Josiah were Amon his father and Manasseh his grandfather. Manasseh reigned for fifty-five years, longer than any other king of Israel or Judah. Amon reigned only two years and was assassinated by his servants. Both of these kings "did that which was evil in the sight of the LORD". Of Manasseh we read that he "made Judah and the inhabitants of Jerusalem to err, so that they did evil more than did the nations, whom the LORD destroyed before the children of Israel" (2 Chronicles 33:9). It seems clear from 2 Kings 23:26 and 24:3,4 that the wickedness of Manasseh was so outstanding that he led the people of God past the point at which God determined to remove them from their place by defeat and captivity. It was against this background that Josiah came at an early age to the throne.

Without the benefit of divine insight, is it possible to imagine a more unlikely situation in which to find the development of the spiritual revival that Josiah pursued? Against the darkness of his time and so near to the final judgement he shines the more brightly in his faithfulness to God and in his single minded determination to put right what had gone wrong in the conduct and service of God's people. From this we may conclude that there is no set of circumstances or spiritual condition of men so unfavourable that God through His servants cannot give deliverance and make evident His glory and His reviving grace.

His Youth

Josiah's grandfather Manasseh died when Josiah was six years old. Although Manasseh did so much evil during his long reign, in his later years he humbled himself and came to know the Lord and His mercy. (2 Chronicles 33:12-19). It is perhaps possible that the repentant old king spent time with his infant grandson and, in the terrible knowledge of his own wasted years, charged the impressionable child with the importance of seeking after the God of David his father. If so, then Josiah greatly profited from the instruction at a time when there must have been little godly teaching,

Josiah was eight years old when he began to reign. At the age of fifteen, he began to seek after God and when he was nineteen he began to remove the many trappings of idolatry and its foul practices from Jerusalem and Judah and also from outside the kingdom of Judah in the cities of the other tribes of Israel. It is worth noting that all of his comprehensive work of reform and restoration in the things of God was set in motion by the time he was twenty six. Here is one of the most outstanding examples in the Scriptures of the power of a young life spent in the Lord's service.

There are three lessons we may derive:

(1) In the things of God there is no substitute for a well-spent youth.

(2) It is never too early to start.

(3) The importance of teaching very young people the ways of God cannot be over-emphasized.

The House and The Book

When Josiah was twenty-five he turned his attention to the condition of the house of God and set in hand a programme of repair. Here is another example of Josiah walking "in all the ways of David his father". It was David who said, "I dwell in a house of cedar, but the ark of God dwelleth within curtains" (2 Samuel 7:2), thus earning the divine commendation "Whereas it was in thine heart to build an house for My Name, thou didst well ..." (1 Kings 8:18).

The work of repair in the house of God gave rise to a very important discovery. Hilkiah the priest found in the temple the book of the law of the Lord. It had been lost for a long time through the carelessness and wilful neglect of kings and people. Shaphan the scribe brought this precious find and read it before the king. When Josiah heard the contents he rent his clothes and humbled himself before the Lord. Nearly twenty years later Josiah's son Jehoiakim sat before the fire in his winter house and heard the book of Jeremiah read to him. Jehoiakim's response to the words of God was very different from his father's. When he had heard no more than three or four columns Jehoiakim took the roll from the reader, cut it to pieces with a knife, and burned it in the fire. This contrast with Josiah, broken and weeping because of the words of God, brings to mind the message of the Lord through Isaiah, "to this man will I look, even to him that is poor and of a contrite spirit, and that trembleth at My word" (Isaiah 66:2).

We may therefore conclude that, in the matter of spiritual revival among the people of God, concern for the house of God is a vital ingredient, and humble and contrite attentiveness to the Word of God is all-important.

The Leader and the People

Josiah displayed great strength of purpose in purging the land and the temple of idolatrous effects. This task seems to have taken six years to complete, having involved the destruction of accumulated errors of five centuries. The earliest examples dated even from the reign of Solomon whose alien wives turned away his heart in old age after other gods. 2 Kings chapter 23 provides a catalogue of the religious antiques of human design that the faithful Josiah destroyed. It was all a sad monument to the fatal tendency in men to follow their own wills and deviate from the plain instruction of God. Josiah gave a bold and uncompromising lead in the removal of all this offensive obstruction to the true service of the Lord.

When Josiah sent to inquire of the Lord concerning the words of the book, he was given to understand that the Lord would not go back on His determination to bring judgement on the people and the city. "My wrath is poured out upon this place, and it shall not be quenched". It is significant that the pronouncement of certain judgement did not deter Josiah at all in his efforts to put things right. There was no fatalistic acceptance that nothing was worth changing because doom could not be avoided. He went on to read the book in the ears of the people and with them he made a covenant before the Lord to walk after Him and keep His commandments.

He further emphasized this new beginning by keeping the passover in Jerusalem. The first passover had been kept nearly a thousand years before. It marked a new beginning for Israel when they left Egypt's power and bondage behind forever, and surged out into the wilderness to become a holy nation to the Lord. In the closing years of their freedom as a nation they again kept the ancient feast in all the freshness of the spiritual renewal that Josiah's leadership had achieved. We are told that there was not kept such a passover from the days of the judges that judged Israel, nor in all the days of the kings of Israel nor of the kings of Judah. Why was Josiah's zeal unimpaired by the sombre tidings of certain judgement from the Lord? Surely because his concern for the honour of the Lord was so much greater than any other consideration.

Jeremiah began to prophesy in the year after Josiah began to purge the land, and in his prophesy we have some indication of the true spiritual condition of the people. "The word of the LORD is become unto them a reproach; they have no delight in it" (Jeremiah 6:10). "Judah hath not returned unto Me with her whole heart, but feignedly, saith the LORD" (3:10). We sadly conclude that the spiritual state of the people did not match that of their leader. Echoing down the centuries from a much earlier day of success for Israel come the words of the song, "For that the leaders took the lead in Israel, for that the people offered themselves willingly, bless ye the LORD" (Judges 5:2). For true spiritual prosperity, the leaders must lead but it is essential also for the people to follow.

From all of this we learn that:

> (1) There is no place for compromise in obedience to the Lord's word.

(2) The honour of the Lord's Name is the most important motivation in spiritual revival.

(3) The effect of good leadership can be quickly nullified if the people hold back in their hearts.

The Last Mistake

After all this, when he was thirty nine years old, Josiah made a fatal mistake. He went out and engaged in battle with the king of Egypt without divine sanction and in the face of a warning through the words of Neco from the mouth of God. Before we hasten to describe Josiah as over-confident, careless or forgetful of his need to be dependent always on the Lord, let us soberly reflect on our own lives and take heed. It is a reminder that Josiah was a man of like passions with us. May we learn from his strengths and his failing. Here is the divine assessment of a very great servant of the Lord. "Like unto him was there no king before him, that turned to the LORD with all his heart, and with all his soul, and with all his might, according to all the law of Moses; neither after him arose there any like him". Josiah was the last good king before the coming of Christ and surely that is how he would wish to be remembered.

CHAPTER NINE: THE STIRRING OF A REMNANT

═══

OFTEN THE OLD TESTAMENT with its valuable, heart-stirring truth is neglected, and thus its encouragement and practical lessons are missed. We would encourage readers to persevere in gaining an understanding of the events and the underlying principles in this chapters. To help in this it is suggested that you read the following Bible passages, which are too long to quote in full - 2 Chronicles 36; Jeremiah 25:1-14; 29:1-14; Isaiah 44:28 and 45:7, Daniel 9:1-21; Ezra 1. The following time chart may also help (some authorities may date the years differently but the time span remains approximately the same).

- 712 B.C. (approx.) - Isaiah foretells concerning Cyrus (during Hezekiah's reign).
- 629 B.C. - Jeremiah begins his prophetic ministry in 13th year of Josiah.
- 624 B.C. - Revival in the 18th year of Josiah's reign.
- 610 B.C. - Josiah dies. Jehoahaz reigns for three months. Jehoiakim (Eliakim) begins 11-year reign.
- 606 B.C. - Nebuchadnezzar begins reign in Babylon. 70-year period of captivity begins for Daniel and others.
- 599 B.C. - Jehoiachin reigns three months; goes into captivity. Zedekiah begins 11-year reign.
- 588 B.C. - The temple burnt; Jerusalem laid waste; the

land desolated.

- 536 B.C. - A Remnant (almost 50,000) returns under Zerubbabel.
- 457 B.C. - A further company returns under Ezra.

In the past two chapters, we have considered Hezekiah's faithfulness and Josiah's spiritual leadership. During the reigns of both these kings God foretold events to be fulfilled at the time of this month's subject. Isaiah, in Hezekiah's reign about 175 years before the event, prophesied that a king, Cyrus by name, would be God's anointed servant in a deliverance of His people; and Jeremiah began his prophetic ministry in the thirteenth year of Josiah's reign which led to the remarkable revival in the 18th year (2 Chronicles 34:8-35:19). After Josiah's death Jeremiah's ministry continued about another 23 years when all the kings of that time were unfaithful and evildoers. In the fourth year of Jehoiakim's reign there were some highly significant events. Nebuchadnezzar began his reign as the king of Babylon, and Jeremiah prophesied of a captivity that would last for 70 years, which began that year when a number of Jews including Daniel were taken to Babylon. More Jews were taken captive on successive occasions until the end of Zedekiah's reign. Finally there were only a few poor people left, the rest having died through famine or war or else taken into captivity (2 Kings 25:12).

The Captivity

Although it was only 88 years from the height of Josiah's spiritual revival until the stirring in Babylon of a Remnant who would return to Jerusalem, into those years were pressed unspeakable suffering and sorrow, the fruit of sin. God delayed His judgements but Israel's repeated sin at last brought its fearful consequences. Jeremiah pleaded during the reign of the last king, Zedekiah, but that king "humbled not himself before Jeremiah the prophet speaking from the mouth of the Lord". "All the chiefs of the priests, and the people, trespassed very greatly after all the abominations of the heathen; and they polluted the house of the Lord which He had hallowed in Jerusalem ... until the wrath of the LORD arose against His people, till there was no remedy" (2 Chronicles 36:12-16).

The house of God was burnt and all its vessels and the treasures of the house of the Lord were taken to Babylon where they would one day do service in the drunken revellings of king Belshazzar (Daniel 5:1-4). The book of the Lamentations of Jeremiah reveals the terrors of those days and the prophet says: "For these things I weep; mine eye, mine eye runneth down with water" (Lamentations 1:16). And away in captivity the people learned the awful lesson of separation from the privileges of God's house and service.

"By the rivers of Babylon, there we sat down, yea, we wept when we remembered Zion. Upon the willows in the midst thereof we hanged up our harps. For there they that led us captive required of us words of song, and our tormentors required mirth, saying, Sing us one of the songs of Zion. How shall we sing the LORD'S song in a strange land?" (Psalm 137:1-4 Revised Version Margin).

During the reign of Zedekiah Jeremiah wrote a letter to those Jews who had already been taken captive. He told them to "build houses and live in them ... multiply there, and do not decrease" (Jeremiah 29:4-7 Revised Standard Version). This counsel had not been acceptable to them because they hoped for a quick return to Jerusalem. But the determination of the Lord saw that they did dwell there, and sadly when the Lord's appointed time came for their return only a comparative few were willing to leave their new surroundings and to return to the place of God's choice for His dwelling-place and service. Similarly many of God's children today are comfortable in their religious associations and are unwilling to accept the call and challenge of God's truth concerning His spiritual house.

Divine Movement

The stirring of a Remnant began with the Word of God and with prayer. Daniel is the outstanding example of the exercise that took place in godly hearts. He "understood by the books the number of the years whereof the word of the Lord came to Jeremiah the prophet" (Daniel 9:2). We may reasonably assume those books to be Jeremiah and Isaiah and perhaps 2 Kings. The Word of God led to prayer and Daniel set his face unto the Lord God to seek by prayer and supplications and he made confession in a prayer which is worthy of deepest consideration and emulation (Daniel 9:3-19). This agreed with that which God said through Jeremiah: "When 70 years are completed for Babylon, I will visit you, and I will fulfil to you My promise ... Then you will call upon Me and come and pray to Me, and I will hear you. You will seek Me and find Me; when you seek Me with all your heart" (Jeremiah 29:10-13 RSV).

Thus, as it ever must be, by the Word of God and by prayer there was a revival. God stirred the hearts of faithful men and women (Ezra 1:5) although they were but a remnant of the many who had been carried away and who had increased in numbers during captivity. When their hearts had been prepared then God stirred the heart of the mighty ruler, Cyrus (Ezra 1:1). In his edict he says that the Lord had charged him to build for God a house in Jerusalem. Someone had brought before him the prophecy in Isaiah 44:28-45:7 and we may wonder if Daniel had been the channel of divine working to tell Cyrus what God had said about 175 years previously.

Less than 50,000 people made the long journey to Jerusalem, a small number by comparison with those who had left Egypt (Exodus 12:37,38) almost 1,000 years before. But their hearts were right. The Lord's house and the Lord's song were not to be found in Babylon. There were 128 singers of the children in Asaph as well as 200 singing men and singing women who returned to Jerusalem. The Lord's song belonged to His house and thither would they go. Daniel's heart went back in prayer to the purposes of God in their redemption out of Egypt and he remembered "the law of Moses the servant of God". They were only a few but they longed for the renewal of the divine purpose.

The parallel for today is too obvious and too vital to be neglected. The apostles' teaching which accurately conveyed the mind of the Lord Jesus for the children of God should be the desire of our hearts. "You should remember ... the commandment of the Lord and Saviour through your apostles" (2 Peter 3:2 RSV). There is a spiritual Babylon today, but few are captivated with the prospect and purpose of building God's house according to His will. There is a great need for the study of God's Word by willingly obedient hearts and for prayer of Daniel like character. Dear reader, how precious and how desirable is God's house to you?

Those Who Were Stirred

In Ezra 2 there is a list of many of those who returned. In verses 3-20 they are identified by ancestral names. These are names not previously met in the Scriptures. Others have forfeited their blessings and privileges. But we note that at least nine of these names are repeated in Ezra 8 which is about 80 years later. Better to come to God's house late than not to come at all. But what blessings they missed who hesitated so long to return!

In verses 21-35 they are identified by their places of inheritance. It is good to see 128 from Anathoth, the town of Jeremiah. In verses 36-39 the priests are identified; in verse 40 the Levites; in verse 41 the singers and in verse 42 the porters - each to find a place in divine service in the rebuilt house of God.

In verses 43-54, the Nethinim are identified. These are those who were 'given' to the house of the Lord. We recognize a Canaanite name in Sisera. They were like the men of Gibeon who became "hewers of wood and drawers of water for the house of my God" and "for the altar of the Lord" (Joshua 9:23,27). To such we might have thought that Babylon would be an attraction, freed from obligation in divine things. But no! The precious truth of service in God's house is beyond compare. Far better to fill a lowly place in God's house than to stand tall in Babylon. Such a truth only faith can comprehend.

In verses 55-57 are the descendants of Solomon's servants. Their ancestors had been bondservants but they had been happy under the wisdom of Solomon (1 Kings 9:20, 21; 10:8). The person of the king had been attractive to them and his blessings rich, and 450 years later these things still influenced understanding hearts.

We can somewhat imagine the earnest conversations of the godly Israelites in their houses in Babylon and how lovingly and longingly they had spoken concerning the place of the Name, God's house in Jerusalem, when we consider that 7,337 of their servants went up with them to begin a new life in hardship and yet in blessing. They left Babylon because the highways to Zion were in their hearts (Psalm 84:5). Happy people!

Shortage of space prevents a more comprehensive study of this Revival but may our spiritual appetite be stirred to meditate in this precious joyful truth which has a priceless message for us. May our eyes be opened to behold wondrous things which have a parallel for ourselves today.

———————————

CHAPTER TEN: PROPHETS OF REVIVAL

———

REVIVAL! GODLY MEN in darkened days have always longed for it! The cry of Habakkuk in a time of impending judgement was: "O Lord, revive Thy work in the midst of the years, in the midst of the years make it known" (Habbakuk 3:2). Ezra acknowledged the grace of God in bringing from captivity a remnant with a nail in His holy place ... reviving to setup the house of God (Ezra 9:8,9). Revival is stones from the rubble (Nehemiah 4:2); it is the bringing forth of grain and wine after the unfruitfulness of winter (Hosea 14:7); it is the lifting of the humble spirit and the contrite heart (Isaiah 57:15). Our own souls long for it.

Yet adversaries without, apathy among many believers, and an unsympathetic environment all diminish its probability. In days much like our own, God reminded the people through two prophets, Haggai and Zechariah, that He was the One able to shake heavens and earth and to pour down blessing upon His people.

The year was 520 B.C. Fourteen years previously under Zerubbabel's direction the foundation of the house of God had been laid. Then Cyrus of Persia died in 529 B.C. and an unsympathetic Ahasuerus came to power and lent an ear to Samaritan counsellors who convinced him that work on the temple should be suspended. In 520 B.C., what should have been a glorious house lay waste, overgrown with weeds and scarred by debris. Crop failure and economic recession caused the people to consolidate their financial position to secure personal comfort, but this brought neither contentment nor divine approbation. Lack of blessing both temporal and spiritual was accepted with gloomy resignation. In the midst of this, God gave four clear messages through Haggai in a period of four months and supplemented those with a series of visions and promises through his contemporary, Zechariah, all to the same intent: build the house; I am with you; I will bless you. Haggai's two chapters are delightfully simple and straightforward; Zechariah's fourteen are far-reaching and complex, but both contain a message for Israel and for our own age about the subject of revival (Romans 15:4).

The command of God had not changed: "Whosoever there is among you of all His people, his God by with him, and let him go up to Jerusalem which is in Judah, and build the house of the Lord" (Ezra 1:3); nor had any the authority to change that word no matter what the circumstance. The commandment was the more important because of the soon coming of the Lord Jesus Christ, to which Haggai alludes in 2:7,9, "the desire (Authorized Version) of all nations shall come ... the latter glory of this house shall be greater than the former" ... (While arguments have surrounded these verses as to whether Messiah's coming to His temple is meant, all things considered I read the verses in that way).

This commandment to build is a reflection of the commission of the Lord Jesus to His disciples in Matthew 28:19. "Go ye therefore" was Haggai's message, and the Lord's. And once again the blessed pope, even the appearing of our great God and Saviour Jesus Christ lends urgency to our obedience. Unfortunately, a "day of small things" led the people to say that it was not the right time to build the house. Haggai's four-fold message instructs all, whether hampered by prevailing philosophy or misinterpretation of Scripture. The house is to be built.

The first communication invites Israel to a consideration of their present state, an evaluation of living without due thought to divine commandment, the result of which is always much labour, little benefit. The second pleads with the people to realize that God is with them, and is reminiscent of that later, "Lo, I am with you alway". God was with them by covenant (2:5); His Spirit abode among them and His promise remained sure, reiterated for our own benefit in Hebrews 12:26,27: "now He hath promised, saying, Yet once more will I make to tremble not the earth only, but also the heaven. And this word, Yet once more, signifieth the removing of those things that are shaken, as of things that have been made, that those things that are not shaken may remain. Wherefore receiving a kingdom that cannot be shaken, let us have thankfulness (RVM), whereby we may offer service well-pleasing unto God with reverence and awe: for our God is a consuming fire". Haggai's third message reminds us that mere working on a holy project does not in itself make one holy. Association with dead works always renders one unclean.

Thank God for repentance from dead works and the blood of Christ which cleanses the conscience from dead works, that in our day we may serve the living God. Our engagement in the building of God's house puts God under no obligation to bless.

It is in His abounding grace that He deigns to use the efforts of men and to give the promise of any present or future blessing. Haggai's fourth message is directly to Zerubbabel, yet shows us in him God's greater Leader. Zerubbabel was to be God's signet, His sign of authority in that day; in the present and in days shortly to unfold will the signet of God be impressed upon men through His greater Leader, for He is yet to be glorified in His saints and marvelled at in them that behaved (2 Thessalonians 1:10).

Between Haggai's second and third messages, Zechariah began to amplify what Haggai had been saying, particularly in Zechariah 1 to 8. In the following chapters we are taken far beyond temple-building days of the past to future ultimate triumph in Israel under Christ, when all to do with Israel will be holy unto Jehovah. It would seem that the visions of the first eight chapters of Zechariah came all in one night (Zechariah 1:7), just five months after the rebuilding of the temple had been resumed. The first shows the divinely ordained interest of heavenly beings in earthly things, especially in things to do with the building of the house of God. Hebrews 1:14 tells us that this same interest obtains today.

The second and third visions promise divine intervention in the nations so that God's purposes might be carried out and His servants protected, a matter which finds concurrence both in relation to the words of Moses in Deuteronomy 32:8 for Israel in the past, and to Paul's in 1 Corinthians 3:16,17 for God's people in this age. The calling out and together of a people and the furnishing of that people for the fulfilment of divine service is ever a priority item with God. Joshua, high priest over a covenanted people is to be reclothed in vision four, and the Old Covenant still in effect, renewed through the cleansing of people and priesthood, but points forward to the new one under which we now serve.

Christ is a priest of good things now come, through the greater and more perfect tabernacle (Hebrews 9:11), and God's people are seen together in sanctification of the Spirit, unto obedience and the sprinkling of the blood of Jesus Christ (1 Peter 1:2). Notice for interest the nine times in the book of Hebrews where the Lord is called Jesus, the same name as Joshua, this Old Covenant high priest.

Vision five shows an earth-based witness (compare Revelation 1:20) into which fruit-bearing branches, "sons of oil", become channels which receive from the Lord beside whom they stand and pour forth that which is received to the sustaining and brightening of the testimony. Whatever all the explanations of the sixth vision of scroll and ephah might be, one thing is very clear. What is described by the angel as wickedness and associated with the curse has no place in the house of God. Wickedness pertains to Babylon and must be delivered there. Vision seven again emphasizes the working of the great powers in heaven in the fulfilling of divine purpose upon the earth; shows the triumphant crowning of Joshua the high priest, reflecting the victory of the Lord in the re-establishing of His people; and finally points forward to the Branch, who in a yet future day will build the temple of Jehovah.

The visions given to Zechariah by an unchanging God along with the four messages through Haggai should speak great encouragement to God's people who long for revival in our day. We must consider our ways; cleanse ourselves from all defilement of flesh and spirit, perfecting holiness in the fear of God (2 Corinthians 7:1); and build the house, ever aware of God's interest, presence and power with us. Words such as, "I am with you", "he that toucheth you toucheth the apple of His eye", "I will take pleasure in it (the house), and I will be glorified, saith the LORD", should urge us on to a fulfilment of His purposes in us. God "willeth that all men should be saved, and come to the knowledge of the truth" (1 Timothy 2:4).

CHAPTER ELEVEN: BACK TO THE BOOK

===

"AS THOU KNOWEST NOT what is the way of the wind ... even so thou knowest not the work of God who doeth all" (Ecclesiastes 11:5). The way of the wind, or (Revised Version margin) the spirit: the Hebrew word 'ruach' is translated either wind or spirit, even when speaking of the Spirit of God. Similarly in John 3:8 the same word 'pneuma' is used both for the wind and the Spirit. "The wind bloweth where it listeth, and thou hearest the voice thereof, but knowest not whence it cometh, and whither it goeth: so is every one that is born of the Spirit".

When God has brought reviving among His people, it has always been the fruit of the Spirit's work. He has come silently, and suddenly, in power and great glory to God; and when He has gone few ever discerned from whence He had come, far less whither He had gone.

The Spirit is sovereign in the choice of those who will be in the path of the wind of revival as it begins to blow. We have considered in previous issues some of the choices in the days when the quickening wind swept through Judah and Benjamin. It would take a long and separate essay to consider the men and women in every era whose manner of life has been influenced by the initial movements of the Spirit in His quickening power.

Ezra - the Man

Suffice it for this present chapter to examine briefly the spiritual dedication of one particular man whom the Spirit used in this way, if perchance something of his Spirit-used qualities may become powerful in us.

It will be more profitable in our short study to consider the positive side of Ezra's devotional life, rather than become involved in the historical problems of where to place him in relation to Nehemiah, and the sequence of events in post-captivity Judah and Jerusalem generally.

The exercised remnant of around some 50,000 souls returned to Judah from Babylon as narrated in Ezra 1. Their subsequent experiences were dealt with in our two previous chapters. From Ezra 7, we learn that the man Ezra himself returned with some 1,500 others. His return was actually a commission from Artaxerxes, the king in Babylon, to make enquiries as to the state of the people in Judah, and to carry a gift of great value for the service of the house of God in Jerusalem.

The Spirit directs us to several points which give early indication that here was a man in the line of His purpose - a man in the path of the wind. He was a priest, a direct descendant of Aaron, through Phinehas who held the covenant of the priesthood. In practice he was a scribe of skill, whose main aim in life was "to seek the law of the ~ and to do it, and to teach in Israel statutes and judgements". Here surely was a man with his priorities right in life - a searcher after the counsels of God so that he might first himself do them and then be thus in a position to teach others to pursue them. He was also a man of known integrity, whom a heathen monarch could trust implicitly.

Journey to Jerusalem

By the riverside Ezra surveyed the exercised group willing to journey with him. His discerning eye was quick to detect the absence of the sons of Levi. So he sent back word to men of influence that ministers were needed for the house of God. In due course they arrived and "according to the good hand of our God upon us" (a choice recurring phrase in the Ezra story) several excellent men were among them.

They were now ready for the long journey, and the mark of the Spirit on the man again revealed itself. There were dangers in the way. They carried great treasure. But such was his confidence in God that he could not think to ask a guard of the king. Here was a man who knew his God and trusted Him.

At the river Ahava he called for a fast, for a time of humbling of heart, for a season of waiting on God. Here was a man of prayer. Then, to twelve of the priests and ten of their trusted brethren, he measured out by recorded weight the precious wealth and vessels for the house of God in Jerusalem, with the memorable words, "Watch ye, and keep them, until ye weigh them at Jerusalem". Here was a man who could trust men of a like spirit.

Mixed Marriages

Reaching Jerusalem, his very presence there "furthered the people and the house of God". But he found the condition of the people completely at variance with the law of God He loved. "Is it not", said Moses in his day, "... that Thou goest with us, so that we be separated, I and Thy people, from all the people that are upon the face of the earth?" (Exodus 33:16). But the earlier spiritual quickening of the remnant had fast died away. It had happened so often before, "O Judah ... your goodness is as a morning cloud, and as the dew that goeth early away" (Hosea 6:4). The people had mingled and married with the many surrounding nations, embracing their evil practices which were an abomination to the Lord. All evidence of separation in the holy nation seemed to have gone. The story is told in Ezra 9.

This man of the Spirit assessed the situation. It roused in him deep righteous anger and sorrow; and he sat down in almost unbelieving astonishment at "the trespass of them of the captivity". The godly in Jerusalem, who feared the name of the Lord and trembled at His word, came along, heartened him, and sat down alongside him. They sat till the hour of the evening sacrifice. Then the man of God rose with his garments rent, fell upon his knees, cast himself before and upon the Lord, and spreading out his hands revealed the kind of man he was in the confession which he made.

Turning Point

This proved to be the turning point; the appalling spiritual declension was again stayed. Here was a true son of Phinehas (Numbers 25). The mourner from the river Ahava led the people into national mourning. His proclamation throughout all Judah and Jerusalem brought the people to the city within three specified days. And there in the broad place before the house of God this great spiritual leader called on the nation to put away the wives which, altogether contrary to the law of God for His own people, they had taken from the surrounding nations. Then the great rain fell, very real at the time but also remarkable in its symbolism. The Spirit's revival of the nation was now under way.

Some twelve years passed between the foregoing incident in Ezra 10 and Nehemiah chapters 1-8. They are silent years in the divine record, faithful Ezra doubtless keeping priestly watch over the people of God. One further consolidation was necessary, the wall had to be rebuilt. Once again God had a man of prayer in readiness, and from Babylon He brought up Nehemiah to be governor in Jerusalem, a worthy team-mate for Ezra. His courageous zeal for "the welfare of the children of Israel" provided all the stimulus of leadership needed by the people. In response to his great rallying call, "Remember the Lord", the people gave without reserve their labour and their money and the wall was rebuilt in fifty-two days.

The Book

Nothing could now hinder the coming of the great day. The people, freshly renewed in their separation, gathered as one man before the Water Gate, as though anticipating the cleansing power of the Word. They called on Ezra to "bring the book of the law of Moses". Bring the Book! Back to the Book! The Spirit of God was in control. The man He had been training and using was now to be instrumental in the quickening of the nation.

It was the first day of the seventh month. A pulpit was erected for Ezra. There in the early morning he took his stand, radiant in revival, flanked by godly men. The whole congregation stood to attention, men and women who could hear with understanding.

He opened the Book and everyone stood up. He blessed the Lord, the great God, and all the people said, Amen, Amen, lifting their hands, bowing their heads to the ground in worship. Then till midday they read aloud the words of the Book and everyone listened attentively. They read, not just any way, not just a jumble of words, but reverently. They read distinctly, interpreting the Hebrew words where necessary to a people many of whom had been born in Babylon and to whom the Book had in any event ceased to be familiar.

Revival

The revival was showing itself in a weeping, broken-down people. You read of it in Nehemiah 8. Then Ezra the priest, Nehemiah the governor, and the Levites who taught the people, wiped away gently the nation's repentant tears. "And all the people went their way, to eat, and to drink, and to send portions, and to make great mirth, because they had understood the words that were declared unto them".

So back of that spiritual revival was Ezra, the man of the Spirit, the man of the Book, the man of example, the man of trust, of prayer, of loyalty, of tears, of command. Well did the Holy Spirit say through Paul, albeit in another context, "think on these things."

CHAPTER TWELVE: REVIVAL IN REMNANT TIMES

ONE OF THE GREAT REVIVALS in the long and fateful history of Israel began when Nehemiah arrived in Jerusalem from Persia, on leave from his position as cup bearer to Artaxerxes the king. According to one chronology, he came 91 years after the first expedition under Zerubbabel in 536 B.C. and 70 years after the temple was completed. It seems hard to believe that more than two generations after the temple foundation was laid the walls of Jerusalem were in ruins.

The Man

Nehemiah, whose name means, "the Lord consoles", came out of a most unlikely place, the royal court of Persia, to cross 700 miles of desert, and in 52 days completed the task of rebuilding the walls. Two months earlier, if the Jerusalem news media had told the people the wall of the city would be up in less than 60 days, they would have said, Impossible! Someone has said, "we have lost the eternal youthfulness of Christianity, and have aged into calculating manhood. We seldom pray in earnest for the extraordinary, the limitless, the glorious. We seldom pray with any confidence for any good to the realization of which we cannot find a way. And yet we suppose ourselves to believe in an Infinite Father". Do we dare to ask of God the things which to men are impossible? "Is anything too hard for the LORD?" (Genesis 18:14).

"Faith, mighty faith, the promise sees

And looks to God alone,

Laughs at impossibilities,

And cries, "It shall be done".

Nehemiah moved along the path of unwavering faith in the power of God, and however and wherever he got his early training, he was God's man for the seemingly impossible. From the chronology we have followed, Nehemiah must have been born either in Babylon or Persia. Of his background we know but little. His occupation was in the royal court of Persia. He was the son of Hachaliah, and it is very unlikely that he had ever seen Jerusalem or the former temple. We conclude this because of Nehemiah's late arrival in the city. However, Psalm 87 tells of those born in Babylon as being in affectionate remembrance by the Lord. "I will make mention of ... Babylon. The Lord shall count, when He writeth up the peoples, this one was born there". We can picture Nehemiah in his off-duty hours poring over the word of God through Moses' writings, while in his heart grew a love for his God, and the place where He had put His Name.

Cupbearers in Eastern courts were said to be men of high calibre who held positions of influence. God had His man, learning in His school while he served a Persian monarch. He was a statesman and reformer of exceptional character and ability, God's man for the hour. Revival was born in tears, in night watches on his knees away in that foreign land. God's house and Jerusalem were written on his heart, and when he heard the news of the broken walls and gates, he "wept, and mourned certain days; and ... fasted and prayed before the God of heaven" (Nehemiah 1:2-4). The flesh could reason, 'Why should I forsake the luxury of the world's greatest empire, and travel the desert to identify with a broken down city, and a remnant of despised people who don't care if the wall is up or down?'

Elements of Revival

Nehemiah's concern was not only for the rebuilding of the wall and repairing the gates to beautify the city, but for the greater vision of restoring the glory of the divine institutions God had given His people for their preservation and separation. He knew it was a crucial moment of their history, and that God was also watching over His Messianic promise in Judah's royal line, latent in the favoured tribe. He knew the high destiny of Judah who carried the holy seed of their Messiah across dark and troubled years until the ancient prophecy be fulfilled. "The sceptre shall not depart from Judah, nor the ruler's staff from between His feet, until Shiloh come; and unto Him shall the obedience of the peoples be" (Genesis 49:10).

Nehemiah went straight to the basic cause of Judah's problem and identified himself with it. "We have dealt very corruptly against Thee, and have not kept the commandments, nor the statutes, nor the judgements" (Nehemiah 1:7). "Very corruptly" - strong words! In his deep perception of the problem he knew this cancer had to be cut out, to save the nation. In earlier years Isaiah had put his finger on a similar problem and a social evil in the nation. "Behold, in the day of your fast ye find your own pleasure, and oppress all your labourers (RVM) ... ye fast ... to smite with the fist of wickedness ... Is not this the fast that I have chosen? To loose the bonds of wickedness, to undo the bands of the yoke?" (Isaiah 58:3-6). In his later reforms, Nehemiah deals with this very problem. It was the extortion that wealthy Jews were guilty of toward their poor brethren, who were forced to mortgage their lands and houses to buy corn. When they could not repay, the lenders foreclosed on the mortgages and took their lands for payment. Chapter 5 records the quick, incisive action of Nehemiah to remedy the problem.

Three days after Nehemiah's arrival in Jerusalem he toured the wall by night. "I arose in the night, I and some few men with me: neither told I any man what my God put into my heart to do for Jerusalem ... and the rulers knew not whither I went, or what I did" (Nehemiah 2:12-16). Some could easily label this as independence. Even Ezra does not appear to have been consulted. This man had never been in Jerusalem before. What authority did he have? The utter neglect he witnessed was appalling to a man who knew what the wall represented in terms of God's purpose in separation. In such irregular times God planted His reformer in the middle of the problem with credentials no one could argue with. His message was incisive and challenging. "Ye see the evil case that we are in, how Jerusalem lieth waste, and the gates ... burned ... come and let us build up the wall of Jerusalem, that we be no more a reproach. And I told them of the hand of my God which was good upon me" (Nehemiah 2:17-18).

It was a rude awakening, and whether or not his hearers liked the man or his methods, he was a leader and his word had power. It has been said that a good leader is one who gets people to do things they don't like, and to enjoy doing them.

Objectives

As soon as the sound of the workmen was heard on the wall, Satan had his activists mocking and threatening to stop the work. When there is no life or movement for God there is no conflict with Satan. He rarely attacks a worldly Christian or a dead church, but any signs of life are signals for him to move in and destroy. Nehemiah had the courage to talk back to the enemies of God, and in so doing he talked back to the Devil who was behind men like Sanballat the Horonite. He knew that it was only in God he was any match for Satan. We need to learn that lesson too.

Nehemiah delegated responsibility to skilled men and saw ten gates repaired (Chap. 3) each with its own name and importance to the life of the city, both for cleansing and service. He knew the entrances and exits needed protection to keep the city and the house of God. In 52 days of glorious victory the wall was built in the face of strong opposition from Satan. Never had they worked so hard, or such long hours in the dual role of workman warrior. Never had people, rulers and priests been so happy, for the joy of the Lord was their strength.

Nehemiah was out for perfection in God's building plan, and experienced Satan's opposition. He must have felt in raw contact with the adversary. Living close to the Lord and striving for perfection in His word and work doesn't make a man popular. I have heard Christians say "his standards are too high". God's standards are always high, and never accommodate to human opinion. Nehemiah was a clear thinker in a day of religious confusion. He saw things as God saw them. His conflicts were the Lord's conflicts, lived through His people. He met Satan head on in open conflict and triumphed over him.

Centuries later Peter wrote, "your adversary the devil, as a roaring lion, walketh about, seeking whom he may devour" (1 Peter 5:8). Someone has written that "it is a delightful thing to get close enough to the adversary to hear him roar ... too many Christians never get into lion country". Revelation 12:10,11 tells of Satan the accuser of the brethren hurling accusations before God day and night about Christians. How were these accusations handled? "They overcame him by the blood of the Lamb, and by the word of their testimony; and they loved not their lives unto the death" (Authorized Version). James 4:7 also gives us the Holy Spirit's resource for close range attacks by Satan. "Resist the devil, and he will flee from you".

As a restorer, reformer and revivalist Nehemiah led the people back to God. This is of prime importance in revival. His reforms included the ministry of Ezra bringing the word of God which made the people weep tears of repentance. Nehemiah corrected social evils in the nation. Usury (chapter 5), sabbath merchandising and mixed marriages (chapter 13) all came under the scrutiny of the reformer and were corrected. One thing runs through this man's ministry: he knew the spirit of the word of God, and the people felt its power. Paul wrote, "the letter killeth, but the spirit giveth life". Nehemiah knew such a revolution in his life for the glory and honour of God, and such denial of all self interests that if he had lived in Paul's day, he too could have said, "I am crucified with Christ".

The revivalists and reformers of Israel's fateful days were the prophets who knew God as a consuming fire, and yet a God of infinite compassion. They fell on their faces in holy awe in the presence of His glory and power. They saw their own base sinfulness, and led the nation in repentance and confession of sin. True revival may be summed up in a few words; hunger for God, an awareness of the presence and glory of God in our own lives. Assemblies will not be touched with the power of the Spirit of God until our lives have been touched in the secret place.

Malachi's message struck deep at the root of the remnant's failure, and is as much for God's people today as it was then. "Ye have turned aside ... return unto Me, and I will return unto you saith the LORD of hosts ... Will a man rob God? Yet ye rob Me ... Bring ye the whole tithe into the storehouse ... and prove Me now ... if I will not open you the windows of heaven, and pour you out a blessing that there shall not be room enough to receive it" (Malachi 3:7-10).

ABOUT THE AUTHORS

———

CHAPTER ONE: JOHN DRAIN

CHAPTER TWO: ALAN TOMS

CHAPTER THREE: JIM JOHNSTON

CHAPTER FOUR: MARTIN ARCHIBALD

CHAPTER FIVE: R. LINDSAY

CHAPTER SIX: LAURIE BURROWS

CHAPTER SEVEN: JACK GAULT

CHAPTER EIGHT: JOHN ARCHIBALD

CHAPTER NINE: GEORGE KENNEDY

CHAPTER TEN: ED NEELY

CHAPTER ELEVEN: JACK FERGUSON

CHAPTER TWELVE: BOB ARMSTRONG

Did you love *Great Spiritual Revivals*? Then you should read *An Introduction to Bible Covenants*[1] by Hayes Press!

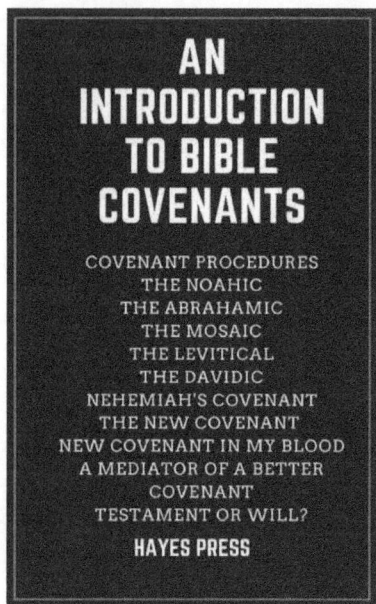

AN INTRODUCTION TO BIBLE COVENANTS

COVENANT PROCEDURES
THE NOAHIC
THE ABRAHAMIC
THE MOSAIC
THE LEVITICAL
THE DAVIDIC
NEHEMIAH'S COVENANT
THE NEW COVENANT
NEW COVENANT IN MY BLOOD
A MEDIATOR OF A BETTER COVENANT
TESTAMENT OR WILL?

HAYES PRESS

[2]

The topic of Bible covenants might seem to be an unusual subject, but it's vitally important to get to grips with to understand how God wants to have a relationship with mankind. This little guide is a perfect way to get a quick introduction to the subject. The first chapter reviews the main components of the Biblical covenant with the following chapters taking a look at the main covenants in the Bible, as well as some lesser well-known ones. The final chapters analyse the progression of these covenants from Old to New Testament,

1. https://books2read.com/u/baPxWx

2. https://books2read.com/u/baPxWx

from the Old Covenant to the New Covenant, and the final chapter concludes the book with a look at the relevance of the use of the word "Testament". Why do we have Old and New Testaments and how is this related to covenants?

Also by Hayes Press

Bible Studies
Bible Studies 1990 - First Samuel
Bible Studies 1991 - The First Letter of Paul to the Corinthians
Bible Studies 1993 - Second Samuel
Bible Studies 1994 - The Establishment and Development of Churches of God
Bible Studies 1995 - The Kings of Judah and Israel from Solomon to Asa
Bible Studies 1992 - The Second Letter of Paul to the Corinthians

Needed Truth
Needed Truth 1888
Needed Truth 2001
Needed Truth 2002
Needed Truth 2003
Needed Truth 2004
Needed Truth 2005
Needed Truth 2006

Needed Truth 2007
Needed Truth 2008
Needed Truth 2009
Needed Truth 2010
Needed Truth 2011
Needed Truth 2012
Needed Truth 2015
Needed Truth 1888-1988: A Centenary Review of Major Themes

Standalone
The Road Through Calvary: 40 Devotional Readings
Lovers of God's House
Different Discipleship: Jesus' Sermon on the Mount
The House of God: Past, Present and Future
The Kingdom of God
Knowing God: His Names and Nature
Churches of God: Their Biblical Constitution and Functions
Four Books About Jesus
Collected Writings On ... Exploring Biblical Fellowship
Collected Writings On ... Exploring Biblical Hope
Collected Writings On ... The Cross of Christ
Builders for God
Collected Writings On ... Exploring Biblical Faithfulness
Collected Writings On ... Exploring Biblical Joy
Possessing the Land: Spiritual Lessons from Joshua
Collected Writings On ... Exploring Biblical Holiness
Collected Writings On ... Exploring Biblical Faith
Collected Writings On ... Exploring Biblical Love

These Three Remain...Exploring Biblical Faith, Hope and Love

The Teaching and Testimony of the Apostles

Pressure Points - Biblical Advice for 20 of Life's Biggest Challenges

More Than a Saviour: Exploring the Person and Work of Jesus

The Psalms: Volumes 1-4 Boxset

The Faith: Outlines of Scripture Doctrine

Key Doctrines of the Christian Gospel

Is There a Purpose to Life?

An Introduction to Bible Covenants

The Hidden Christ - Volume 2: Types and Shadows in Offerings and Sacrifices

The Hidden Christ Volume 1: Types and Shadows in the Old Testament

The Hidden Christ - Volume 3: Types and Shadows in Genesis

Heavenly Meanings - The Parables of Jesus

Fisherman to Follower: The Life and Teaching of Simon Peter

Called to Serve: Lessons from the Levites

Needed Truth 2017 Issue 1

The Breaking of the Bread: Its History, Its Observance, Its Meaning

Great Spiritual Revivals

An Introduction to the Book of Hebrews

The Holy Spirit and the Believer

Exploring The Psalms: Volume 1 - Thoughts on Key Themes

Exploring The Psalms: Volume 2 - Exploring Key Elements

Exploring the Psalms: Volume 3 - Surveying Key Sections

The Psalms: Volume 4 - Savouring Choice Selections

Profiles of the Prophets

The Hidden Christ - Volumes 1-4 Box Set

The Hidden Christ - Volume 4: Types and Shadows in Israel's Tabernacle
Baptism - Its Meaning and Teaching
Conflict and Controversy in the Church of God in Corinth
In the Shadow of Calvary: A Bible Study of John 12-17
Moses: God's Deliverer
Sparkling Facets: Bible Names and Titles of Jesus
A Little Book About Being Christlike
Keys to Church Growth
From Shepherd Boy to Sovereign: The Life of David
Back to Basics: A Study of Core Bible Teaching and Practice
An Introduction to the Holy Spirit
Israel and the Church in Bible Prophecy
"Growth and Fruit" and Other Writings by John Drain
15 Hot Topics For Today's Christian
Needed Truth Volume 2 1889
Studies on the Return of Christ
Studies on the Resurrection of Christ
Needed Truth Volume 3 1890
The Nations of the Old Testament: Their Relationship with Israel and Bible Prophecy
The Message of the Minor Prophets
Insights from Isaiah
The Bible - Its Inspiration and Authority
Lessons from Ezra and Nehemiah
A Bible Study of God's Names For His People
Moses in One Hour
Abundant Christianity
Prayer in the New Testament

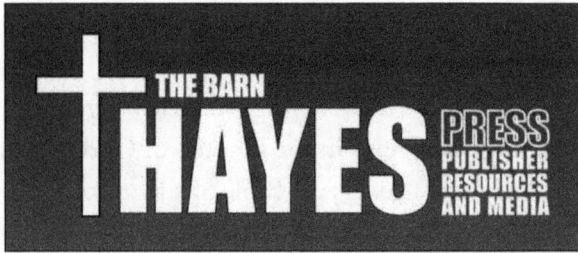

About the Publisher

Hayes Press (www.hayespress.org) is a registered charity in the United Kingdom, whose primary mission is to disseminate the Word of God, mainly through literature. It is one of the largest distributors of gospel tracts and leaflets in the United Kingdom, with over 100 titles and hundreds of thousands despatched annually. In addition to paperbacks and eBooks, Hayes Press also publishes Plus Eagles Wings, a fun and educational Bible magazine for children, and Golden Bells, a popular daily Bible reading calendar in wall or desk formats. Also available are over 100 Bibles in many different versions, shapes and sizes, Bible text posters and much more!

www.ingramcontent.com/pod-product-compliance
Lightning Source LLC
Chambersburg PA
CBHW021135020426
42331CB00005B/783